*This book is dedicated to
all of the beautiful mothers
who are no longer with us.*

*May we always feel their warmth
and encouragement in our hearts.*

LEIGH VAN DER HORST

# without my Mum

NERO

526 853 82 2

Published by Nero,
an imprint of Schwartz Publishing Pty Ltd
Level 1, 221 Drummond Street
Carlton VIC 3053, Australia
enquiries@blackincbooks.com
www.nerobooks.com.au

National Library of Australia Cataloguing-in-Publication entry:
Van Der Horst, Leigh, author.
Without my mum : a daughter's guide to grief,
loss and  reclaiming life / Leigh Van Der Horst.
9781863958363 (paperback)
9781925203998 (ebook)
Van Der Horst, Leigh.
Mothers—Death.
Bereavement.
Mothers and daughters.
155.9370852

Cover photographs by Katie Toland –
www.katietolandphotography.com.au
Cover artwork by Sarah Lord –
www.etsy.com/people/sarahlordpapercuts
Text design & typesetting by Vivid.

# Foreword

Stories animate the human experience. They provide opportunities for self-reflection and connection. When we walk together with the grief that comes with losing a loved one, hearing from others who have travelled along that same path can transform the way we sit with loss.

Stories and grief have long been a part of my professional and personal world. I have spent the last decade supporting people through counseling speaking to groups of people raw with the sadness of catastrophic loss and then writing those stories for others to share. Through my work, I have come to acknowledge that in grief—as in life—there is no rulebook. There are no hierarchies or 'typical' responses when it comes to grief. The reactions of those who are grief-stricken cannot be predicted or planned for. Our life continues on and the sadness becomes part of that action of moving forward.

The way we live our lives cannot be a dress rehearsal for the grief we might endure. Our connection with the person who is no longer here speaks to how much their life impacted the way we continue on with our own after they are gone.

Leigh Van Der Horst embraces the idea that to share the stories of what we endure allows us to be both vulnerable and brave in giving words to the depth of emotion experienced. The stories we tell of our losses can connect people in ways many may not have ever imagined. I had the privilege of speaking to Leigh through the power of social media and the intimacy of Skype. We connected about our shared passion for truthful narratives on life and loss. She shared with me her ideas of living a rich and meaningful life post-loss. How the death of her lovely mum made her turn inwards to explore how grief can change a person—and how that experience continues to touch the way she lives her life as a woman, a partner and a mum.

Grief is not a linear process. There are no stages to be endured or actions to complete as a way of 'successfully' navigating the feeling that follows. Grief stays with people forever, but the sensation—the triggers—that come with a waft of perfume, a song on the radio or even a Mother's Day flower can pull people back into the grief space until they resurface ready to face the world again. And people do face the world again—in their own time, in their own ways.

We live in a world where the concept of complicated or prolonged mourning is seen as an illness. We pathologise the grieving process by seeking ways to label the emotions that we all experience when a loved one is gone. Emotions that are normal, that are valid. There is no 'right way' to grieve. It is impossible to predict how we might react when tragedy strikes, but the power of sharing stories—like the stories that sit within this book—create virtual connections that can help people stop and think 'me too' when the words of another resonate deeply.

Leigh's journalled reflections of rebuilding her life after the loss of her mum, worldwide contributions by other women on that same path of loss and growth, the last section of hopeful reflections on the mothering journey and all points in between—this book as a whole reminds me that there is something undeniably inspiring about other peoples stories. It is comforting to know that life goes on and that in the midst of trauma and sadness, new truths can be learned about who we are and how we cope.

The power of words is a wonderful thing. I hope you enjoy this book for the message of hope it offers and for the virtual rub on the back it gives to those who might need one.

Enjoy.

**Sarah Wayland, PhD**
Grief researcher and Counsellor
*www.sarahwayland.com.au*

## Grief contacts

Lifeline Australia
13 11 14
*www.lifeline.org.au*

Grief Line Australia
1300 845 745
*www.griefline.org.au*

Mensline Australia
1300 78 99 78
*www.mensline.org.au*

As I turned the corner, I suddenly found myself walking behind two men pushing a trolley with an empty body bag on it. It was such a long walk down the white, sterile corridor towards room 17. I didn't think much of the body bag. It was a common sight sadly and I was running on autopilot—I had been for a while. The past week had seen such a decline. Finally I reached her room. There she was. My beautiful mum. Her blankets pulled up to her chin. She must have been getting cold now. The end was near. She looked so peaceful. As I quietly tiptoed in, I breathed in the abundant scent of freshly cut flowers. By now, one would be forgiven for thinking mum's room was a florist shop! She loved flowers and they certainly did cheer up the otherwise morbid impression of her environment. She opened her eyes, so happy to see me. "Hi love", she said with her big, beaming smile. She was all teeth. Cancer had stolen so much from her. 'Hi Mum', I said—barely unable to make eye contact with her for fear of crying—'How are you today?'. She looked gaunt, literally skin and bone. I leant over and gave her a kiss then pulled a chair up nice and close to her and got comfortable. The rest of my day belonged to my Mum. Time was precious. I knew we were going to part soon. I had accepted that I could not change it. I could not cure her. The time to say goodbye forever was drawing near…

# Introduction

I grew up like most lucky Australian girls. I had a loving family, nice (and sometimes not-so-nice) friends, interests in boys, horses, sports, more boys! In my very early years, I revelled in my dad's practical jokes. He was the master! I would come home from school sometimes to an elaborate set up. Dad would involve my dolls in some sort of scenario, often depicting that they had been up to no good. His stories were too funny. He must have devoted a lot of time to setting up various scenes and sometimes—only once or twice—he nearly had me fooled. He could be very convincing when he wanted to be. My dad was the 'fun' guy and my mum was the strict one. Whatever she said was final! Mum was fun too but it seemed that, early on, the roles were set and that's just the way it went. It's funny—as I became older, I looked up to my mum so much more for approval and praise—she was a tough cookie. Even at a young age, my mum's wellbeing was of upmost importance to me. I would always ask her if she was OK. This concern of mine continued right up until her last breath. In fact, even now without her here, I still worry if she is OK.

I drifted from my dad eventually as I grew to become a woman and became closer to Mum. Maybe that's a natural progression—I'm not sure. I have one brother named Jim and we were very close as children. I pretty much wanted to do everything he did. I played in his football team at one point—probably as a way to spy on his cute friends— something that must have driven him mad! I remember running to training with him and always talking non-stop, often in a horrendous baby voice—a bad habit of mine as a young girl. Jim was very patient with me. I have no memories of him getting cross. He was fair and put up with me for a very long time! I do remember though when our relationship changed. He was older and his mates were his world, definitely not his sister. We are good mates now and give each other support when we need it. I can't ask for much more.

As far back as I can remember I had an ongoing issue with self-confidence. I never truly valued who I was. I never felt comfortable in my own skin—someone else's would have been much nicer, I thought. I thrived on drama. Even as young as pre-school, I would pretend to hurt myself so I could wear my arm in a sling! Once I began primary school I was unstoppable. I would throw myself off the climbing frames and land arm first in the hope of breaking a bone or two but—to my disappointment—it never happened. Damn those strong, healthy bones!

When my best friend broke her first—of many to come—bone, I was utterly green with envy. Everyone gave her oodles of attention, which was exactly what I craved. I recall feeling so jealous, especially when everyone gathered around to write and draw on her cast.

I learned from a very young age that if I sulked, I got attention. If something was wrong, people would ask me if I was all right. I grew to see this as a more successful way to get the attention I craved, as opposed to hurting myself. Thus began a long pattern of negative behaviour. It seemed to me that I got what I was looking for. I was not clever enough to understand that I was training my thoughts in a negative way, as well as affecting those around me.

My behaviour throughout my primary school years amounted to a vicious cycle. I was so comfortable being negative that I never realised the adverse reactions of others towards me were due to my own behaviour. This eventuated in a lack of self-love, which made for a hellish journey through high school.

As I gave off a sense of low confidence, I was often targeted by others and made to feel worthless. Like so many young people, I really took this to heart. If only I knew then what I know now! I looked up to the 'dangerous' people and tried my hardest to keep up with them but—fortunately—my inbuilt values would often stop me in my tracks. On the outside I may have looked the part, but inside a war was going on.

I knew the difference between right and wrong and I could never let this go. I also knew that my actions would devastate my parents—especially my mum—and most of the time, this insight thankfully kept me from serious trouble.

All throughout high school—as in primary school—I wished I were someone different. I surrounded myself with like-minded people. I was never challenged to change my behaviour as it suited the group that I spent time with. We were all down in the dumps! I clearly remember people in my school years that smiled and seemed happy, but I just wasn't sure how to become like them. They seemed as though they had it all and I assumed that they must have had better lives than mine. I realise now that the only thing that separated them and myself was attitude. The happy kids had good attitudes—I did not. It was a simple as that—just a different way of thinking and behaving.

I credit my husband for influencing me to begin along a path of positive change in my early 20s. He was one of the most positive people I had met in the years following high school. Thankfully, he was not afraid to let me know when I was out of line and he brought my negative attitude to the forefront—many times! He taught me that life could be so much better if I practiced positive thoughts and behaviour. Bit by bit, I improved as a person. Yet bad habits are hard to break and unfortunately, negative Leigh reigned more often than positive Leigh. So often, the grass still seemed much greener everywhere but within my life. It took a momentous event in the coming years to shape me into the person that I am today. A loss so huge that my entire world crumbled and I was forced to re-build. Here is my story.

# Chapter 1

My husband Tim and I had been married for about two years and the next natural step for us was to start a family. I was ready for a baby, or so I thought. I remember waiting for the birth of my first child like it was yesterday. The phone would constantly ring. Everyone wanted to know if I'd had the baby yet. Often I would answer the phone and be greeted with a disappointed 'Oh hi, you're *still* there then?'. Unfortunately for my dear mother—who was last in a long line of callers one particular day, about six days beyond my due date—she caught me when I was irate. Boy did I let her know it! I did apologise though and reassured her that my husband or I would definitely call when the baby had arrived—but for the moment, I needed to be left alone.

I was waiting. I'd read everything I could about having a baby, feeding a baby, bringing a baby home. In fact I had read so much that I had begun to double up on advice. Physically, I could not have stretched any further and I desperately wanted our much-anticipated first child OUT! Eventually it reached the point where I was 10 days overdue and really wanted to get the show on the road. I went into hospital to be induced one evening but—as there was no progression overnight—I was given an intravenous drip that administered a hormone to start my labour.

I was sitting at the breakfast table—legs spread to allow room for my monstrous belly—enjoying some toast and a cup of tea when the midwife said, 'We've just started the machine so you will feel some twinges soon'. I looked at Tim then shrugged and reassured him that I was fine when suddenly my eyes widened. I dropped the toast, let my cup of tea go cold and started to pace the room. 'Bloody hell!' was all

I could say. Every so often, the midwives would come in and warn me that they were going to increase the intensity of the machine. All I could do was take a deep breath and deal with it. Poor Tim had no idea what to do. As he was always keen for a good old chinwag, he would try to engage me in conversation but each time I would shoot him a 'look'. I'm sure every woman who has given birth knows what I mean by 'the look'. Luckily for him—and me—there was a student nurse in the room and she also loved a chat so he was well occupied as I laboured along.

As this was my first labour, it was my longest. Yet I can't and won't complain as it was all over in just three short hours. Before I knew it—at 11:08am on 2 August 2000—I had our first-born child. A son named Jack. I sat staring at this little baby in a state of shock. As I held our son, I immediately made up excuses for Tim to take him as I was utterly petrified of him. 'What have I done?' I wondered. Jack started to cry and all eyes were fixed on me waiting for me to handle the situation. I had no idea what to do. All that reading went out the door. I had never read anything that said 'You may feel like you want to grab your belongings and run for the hills once your newborn enters the world!'. All of the sweetness and light I had read was useless to me. I felt lost. I was beyond exhausted and I had to pretend—for the following days in hospital—that I was doing great, that I was born to be a mother. Isn't this how we are all meant to react? After all, this was what I had read about and so this was what I tried to portray. It was important to me to appear as though I had it all sorted, that I had control. Never mind the fact that no woman has ever had control over a newborn baby. If anyone was going to win that challenge, then I was sure going to have a damn good crack at it!

Once Jack and I arrived home, Tim lost his wife. The woman he knew vanished for a while and the tired, stressed perfectionist emerged in her stead. When Tim was at work during the day, I would sit—just sit—and wait for Jack to wake or cry. I tried so hard to keep up the pretence of the glowing new mum, but I was so tired. I began to convince myself that I wasn't doing a very good job as a mother. The more exhausted I got, the more down on myself I became. I was so incredibly nervous of Jack that I didn't make myself food for fear of waking him. The phone was unplugged and I just sat—in dead silence—waiting on his every move.

I was the first in our close group of friends to have a baby so—at the time—no-one really knew about post-natal depression. Looking back, it would have done me some good to admit my struggle and get some help. I was my own worst enemy though and would hate for people to know that I found it hard to cope. So I just went on and on, each day following the same bizarre structure. Poor Jack missed out on the special hugs with his mum and the floor time that I had read so much about, where mum lies there gazing lovingly into her amazing little creation's eyes. Instead, he got fed, bathed and put to bed in a military-like routine that no-one dared to upset. Suffice to say, our social life went right out the window!

Things did settle down over time as Jack became a bit older and was easier to handle. I felt safe when I could regain some control over the environment around me. Indeed, I felt semi-human again. I would take Jack on lovely walks in the pram and we had play dates with people who we had met through mothers groups. This contact and companionship became important for my well-being. It was good to spend time with women who were going through the same challenges as me. I never physically hurt Jack during those hard times, but I do feel guilty for all the affection he missed out on in his first couple of months.

When Jack turned one, we bought our first home. It was a lovely weatherboard house in a beautiful bushy area just 10 minutes drive away from my Mum's and Dad's house. We had great plans for this house and were always thinking about how we could improve and modernise it. This was an exciting time for us.

The blissful bubble burst in April 2002, when my Mum and Dad—who had been married for almost 30 years—announced that they were separating. I think it's just as confusing and hurtful for an adult as for a child when their parents split. At least, it felt that way for me. My foundations were being rocked. My parents blamed growing apart as their reason for separating. Sadly, this happens to lots of couples as their children become older. Mum was a very independent lady and my dad relied heavily on her so, when he was on his own, his world just crashed. For quite a while, Tim and I had to pick up the pieces. It took my father a long time to be able to make sound decisions or plans on his own. In the meantime, I became his sounding board.

Eventually, my Dad relocated to the Victorian bushland and tried to piece his life back together. This meant that I rarely saw him but—thankfully—my Mum was still close by.

As we spent more and more quality time together, Mum became my best friend. I learned just how strong she really was. She didn't let the breakdown of her relationship with my father destroy her life or friendships. In fact, she thrived. I'm sure that she would have loved to have had a life partner with who she could happily share things. Mum took the view, however, that if this was the way it had to be then so be it! She made the best of what life gave her and never complained. Her motto was always, 'Life is what you make it'. I was yet to fully understand just what this maxim means.

Our lives were trailing along smoothly and Jack was bringing us joy, so the next natural step for us was to consider trying for another child. Tim always says that he just has to look at me sideways to conceive a child. So, with that confidence spurring us on, we decided it was time. I fell pregnant almost straight away and felt great. After another trouble-free pregnancy, I delivered our second child—another boy—on 24 April 2003.

Beautiful Kye came out with intense force, catching the midwife completely off-guard and almost being dropped as he made his hasty exit. Again, I can't complain about the length of time I was in labour. It was fast and furious like my first but this time lasted only a couple of hours.

During my labour, I went off to 'relax' in the big bath in the birthing ward. Tim helped me in and made sure I was ok. I told him that he would probably get bored so should go and get some lunch. He left with my assurance that I would be there when he had finished. But, about three minutes after Tim left in search of some food, I started getting extreme pain. The transition phase was beginning. I rang the nurse's bell and she came rushing in. Through gritted teeth I mumbled that I was in transition and she helped me out of the bath, gently putting my nightie back on before we made the slow pilgrimage back to my room. As we walked – or hobbled in my case – down the hall, I gripped the wall-mounted handrail tightly and dragged myself along as I winced with pain.

Transition is a really intense phase of labour and presents itself just before you get the urge to push. It's an exciting time for me as it's the sign that baby is very close—but oh the pain. *The pain!*

At the time of my hobble back to my room, a tour of the birthing suite was taking place. I will never forget the looks of horror I received from the newly expectant mums and dads. I wouldn't have been surprised if one of them had dropped to the floor unconscious. Seeing me in the throes of labour was a real awakening for them, I'm sure. But they were not the only ones in for a surprise. As I staggered down the hall, I suddenly saw Tim coming towards me. He smiled and looked rather perplexed as to why I was already out of the bath. Tim told me that he had bought me a magazine in case I was bored. *BORED!* I shot him that look again then quickly muttered that we were at transition stage and pressed ahead eager to reach my room. Once we arrived, I crawled up onto the bed ready to deliver. And that's just what I did!

Poor Kye. He had one bloodshot eye due to the shock of quick labour but, other than that, he was perfect. Though he was smaller than his big brother, Kye looked a lot like Jack and was very peaceful. Indeed, he fitted his name perfectly.

My stay in hospital was calmer this time around as I wasn't so frightened. Mum came straight in with a very proud Jack so he could meet his new brother. He smiled from ear to ear and was very gentle with his little brother. He was instantly in love, as was my beaming mother.

Tim, Jack, Kye and I quickly settled into our new life as a family of four. I remember wondering though how on earth I would be able to look after two children when Tim was at work. How was I going to bath Jack *and* hold Kye? It seemed impossible. I had very little faith in myself. I guess the best way to cope is to be thrown in the deep end and I did just that—I coped.

In the first few weeks of Kye being home, I remember feeling as though I had ruined Jack's life by introducing a new little family member. Sometimes the guilt would make me cry. I would ring Mum and admit my dilemma and she would reassure me that what we had done was a good thing. Mum assured me that it was all right for a child to have to wait for things. In fact, this is sometimes the best solution to toddler tantrums.

I don't know what I would have done without Mum in the very early days of having my babies. Her words were so wise and calming. When I shared how on edge I felt, Mum would remind me that—when she was in my position raising my brother and I—she knew many new mums who were on valium just to smooth out their frenetic days. Being a mother certainly helps you to realise what your own mother went through to bring you up. Suddenly I was so grateful!

At the time when Jack was a toddler and Kye a baby, Mum worked full-time as a teacher. This was work she had done for almost all of my life. I would have loved to have had her around during the week but as this was not an option, we often spent the weekends with her while Tim renovated our home. Mum and I would shop and get coffee together with the kids. She would burp Kye after a feed—a good excuse for a cuddle—and she would teach Jack so many important lessons. The boys loved to visit her house. She would always welcome them with a bickie or a special treat. Freshly made play-doh in Mum's fridge was guaranteed. Plus the boys could rest assured of a lovely collection of toys to play with. The toy troops commanded Mum's spare room and the cot was always beautifully made up, all ready for a tired child to nap. Mum's home was casual, welcoming and very relaxed. I loved to be there too. It was my home away from home.

During our times together, Mum and I would chat about everything. She would reassure me that I was doing the best job that I could. I would often watch the way she was with my boys and remember precious moments from my own childhood. When I was with Mum I always felt safe.

Despite such wonderful support, however, I did continue to have low self-esteem. I would often put too much pressure on myself—and Tim and the boys for that matter. I still believed that life could be better than it was. Poor Tim heard my moans about moving to far-away places and my dreams of travelling somewhere we could never afford to go. I was never happy with what I had. I still lacked confidence in myself. Decision-making was hard for me and I harassed Tim to the point that he never quite knew what grand plan would be next. Looking back, I think that I attempted to reach for such high goals because deep down I knew that they were unattainable. For some reason, it just felt good to create conflict and see how far I could push things. To this day, I am just so impressed with Tim's staying ability and his patience. He knew that there was a good, sound, strong person in there somewhere and I guess he could see something in me that I was yet to discover myself.

With Tim working in a secure job, we decided that the third child we had always planned for was due to be 'ordered'. Again, this was no hard task and—not long after our decision was made—I was pregnant once more. Yet this pregnancy was different to the others as I was so sick. I was sure we were having a girl. We thought it would be a good idea to find out the sex of the baby. We welcomed a boy or girl, but this would be our last child and—if we were having another boy—we needed time to get used to the idea of 'my three sons'.

At 4:05 am on 18 January 2005, our third boy—Joshua—was born! He was the dearest little thing. Born at nine pounds, he was quite a bit bigger than Jack and Kye. He was dark like Tim and had his Poppy's nose. Like his brothers when they were born, he was so peaceful.

Joshua proved his talent immediately as he 'found' his food source straight away and breastfed like a pro. I was relieved that I had been through my last labour, which was again a quick one. Tim likes to relay the story of Josh's birth as he finds it rather amusing that I let him sleep on the hospital couch while I huffed and puffed through the labour. A midwife kindly woke him just as I was about to deliver and he was rather surprised. But I knew by this point that all of the hard work was up to me and I may as well do it myself. Tim has been very supportive with each labour but—truth be told—there's not much the poor men can do to help, so I took the pressure off him this time.

A phone call was made to Mum after we studied Josh's bits and pieces and she was relieved to hear our delivery was safely over. Mum was at our house overnight with Jack and Kye and planned to bring them in later that morning. It's funny but, by the time I found myself with baby number three, I was so calm. I had gained confidence in what I was doing. I was happy to sit and nuzzle my new son and give him everything he needed. I guess that I was a few years older now and with that I felt more womanly and motherly. No longer did I feel like a girl trying to look like a woman and mother – I was a woman and mother. It all felt so natural. I even entertained the thought of just one more baby…

Visiting hours saw Jack and Kye come crashing in with my dishevelled Mum. It was quite a sight. Both boys were mesmerised by Josh. Kye really was still a baby himself and could not quite make out what was going on. But if Jack seemed happy then that was enough for Kye! My mum was teary and had that same 'proud as punch' look that I'd seen her wear when each of my babies arrived. She would just gaze in awe of them. Mum was so proud of what I had achieved. She would scrutinise our babies' features, saying how they had my mouth, Tim's nose, my ears and so on. With Josh, however, there was no question of who he looked like. He was all Tim!

Josh and I came home after just one night and he slotted right in. I recall that his first day at home was a Melbourne scorcher. As temperatures hit about 43 degrees, all the blinds were shut and the air conditioner was going non-stop. But Josh didn't seem to care. Jack and Kye were so excited to have their new brother home. They were beetroot-faced all day as they ran about outside to let off some steam then tore back inside to make sure Josh was still there. It was an early insight into life with three energetic young boys!

I drifted along in a state of utter exhaustion. There was no time to ponder how I would tackle three children—I just took the huge plunge! Jack began his pre-school year and I became a chauffeur, housemaid and all those other hats mums wear. If I wasn't feeding Josh, I was changing Kye's nappy. If I wasn't mopping up spilt drinks and food off the floor, I was back in the car with toddler Kye and baby Josh to drop off or pick up Jack. I was shopping, cooking, cleaning and negotiating tantrums—all with three children. Often I felt like *I* wanted to have a turn at screaming and stamping my foot to get my own way. Wouldn't it be wonderful if we could hit the floor like a bag of spuds and cry if we weren't happy with the way things were going? If only!

Chaos became a natural state of life. Mum would help out whenever she could. She made sure that my freezer was constantly stocked with home-cooked meals, which was a true lifesaver. I had some great friends who were in the exact same parenting stage as me, which was comforting. We would often be in hysterics over the manic state of our lives. Our sleep deprivation sometimes made us do foolish things like running the odd red light, forgetting a child or two when it was time to leave a venue, calling our husbands by our dog's name and so on.

On the whole, I was living the dream life. I was married to a wonderful man and I had three beautiful healthy boys. Life should have felt perfect—but I could not find peace within. I still behaved very selfishly. All I really cared about was myself, until a knock on the door shook my world and changed my life forever.

# Chapter 2

8th March 2005

I'm devastated and so scared. We had some sad news last night. Mum came over at 10pm to tell us that she has bowel cancer. I'm hoping she will be ok. I don't know much about the type of cancer that she has—or any cancer really—but I'm sure it can be fixed. It's not in my plan to lose her early...

On a warm March evening in 2005, there was a knock at the door. I had finally put baby Josh to bed and settled on the couch. Tim got up to answer the door and to my surprise, Mum walked in. I could see her from where I was sitting and I could tell that something was wrong. Mum looked pale and frightened—a look I had never seen her wear before. I stood up, gulped and asked what was wrong. She told me that she had cancer. All of the blood in me drained to my feet. In disbelief, we hugged immediately. I could not believe what I was hearing. My mum—who was so careful of what she ate, who regularly walked and did yoga, who loved every inch of her life—had cancer at age 52.

We sat and talked and cried. Tim made us cups of tea. Mum explained to me that she had bowel cancer. It could be operated on and the outlook was quite good. They may have to do chemotherapy but only time would tell. The good news was they had found it at the right time. I tried to listen to the details but it was as though my ears had shut down their capacity to hear. The sound of my charging heart took over instead. I was in shock. After explaining the situation to me, she embarked on a long drive to break the sad news to her brothers and sister.

I felt numb. My foundations had been rocked for the first time. My mum was never sick. She always worked hard and she never complained. For the first time, I had witnessed my mum look vulnerable. All of my life up to this point, my mum was a confident, strong, very focused and driven woman. I was uncomfortable with her new vulnerability. It was something that I was definitely going to have to get used to.

16th March 2005

Mum had her operation yesterday and the doctor was really confident that he got all of the cancer out – thank God! I saw her last night and she looked quite well, considering. I'm sure she will be sore for a while but we are all relieved that it is over. Thank God she will be OK! I couldn't bear losing my mum.

Mum underwent surgery and it really knocked her around. It was major surgery. The doctors cut out some of her bowel to remove the tumour. My aunty stayed with Mum and looked after her at home. I would have loved to help, but with the boys it was really difficult. Mum became rather unwell for a while and I couldn't bring them over much. I did what I could though. My heart ached to see her struggle to get better. She rapidly lost weight and was so tired. My aunty fed Mum healthy soups and gave her support and company without smothering her. Once Mum was strong again, she went back to work. We all believed that we could put the revolting disease behind us. Life continued on as though nothing bad had happened—until we got our second round of bad news.

*24th March 2005*

*Mum needs chemotherapy. The cancer has spread to her lymph nodes. I'm so scared. I have no idea what any of this means but I'm positive it's not good. I'm completely shocked. People keep saying 'I'm sure she will be ok' and I'm sick of hearing it. She might not be! What if she isn't going to be ok? Then what will I do? I saw her yesterday and she looked terrible, so pale and thin. I hope so much that she will be ok. She just has to be. I'm too young to not have a mum. I need her here with me.*

Mum's cancer had spread and a course of chemotherapy was recommended. At first Mum was not sure whether or not she wanted to have any treatment. It scared her so much. The decision as to whether to undergo chemo was left entirely up to her and thankfully she decided to give it a go. Mum took long service leave from her teaching job and began her chemo cycle.

It's very hard to watch someone go through the motions of chemotherapy. Mum's schedule was one week of medication followed by two weeks of recovery. The week that she had the filthy stuff was ok. But the following week would cause vomiting, extreme fatigue, diarrhoea, painful mouth ulcers, itchy skin, lack of appetite and no energy. By week three, Mum would slowly come good only to start the process again. It broke my heart. Just before the dreadful reaction from the medication would hit, we would head out to shop, have coffee and do normal things that normal mothers and daughters do. One particular time, Mum felt a bit sick. She had to run off through the shopping centre holding her mouth, desperately trying to reach the toilets to vomit. So many people stopped and stared. Jack and Kye were horrified and demanded to know why Nanny was sick. I had to pull together all of my strength to be calm for them and just play it down. All the while I wanted to tell the onlookers to mind their own business then run after my beautiful mum.

As time went on, Mum lost her hair. This was very hard for her. She was never vain about her hair, but she much preferred having it on her head. Bit by bit, Mum's hair came out. She clung on to what she had for as long as she could until, one day, she asked me to shave what was left. I was happy to do that for her in the privacy of her own home. Mum dealt with this as I'd seen her commonly deal with things that were out of her control—with courage and grace. It was bittersweet having Mum home a lot. There were enjoyable times where she got to spend precious time with the boys and I loved having her home for my own selfish reasons. There were many hard times too though. When she was sick, I generally left Mum alone as that is what she wanted.

Mum continued her treatment as per her oncologist's orders until she was given the 'all clear' in October 2005. She would have to have six-monthly check-ups for a while but we were all so thrilled that the imminent threat had gone. Mum went back to work—I went back to being a mum. Life went back to normal. Mum had beaten cancer. Or so we thought.

# Chapter 3

Almost one year to the date since Mum's previous diagnosis, bad news once again arrived.

19 April 2006

Well, again I have been reminded that there are no guarantees in life. Mum came over last night with the devastating news that she has very aggressive liver cancer. She has been told that she will have two to three good months and then her health will rapidly decline. I've never cried so much in my life! I'm so angry and sad. How did this happen? I thought Mum had beaten the bastard disease. I can't believe that she may not be here for next Christmas let alone never see my boys grow up. Why her? Why MY mum? She does not deserve this shit! I don't deserve this. Oh my gosh, my boys need her in their lives. There is so much that they still have to share. There are so many years that I need to share with her. She is so strong and says that she is not afraid to die. I'm not so confident. I can't fathom her dying—it just can't be true. I have to make the most of the time left and leave nothing unsaid. Everything has changed. EVERYTHING feels different. I *feel sick to my stomach. It's just not fair. I have to try to be strong for her...*

On a warm April day, Tim arrived home from work earlier than usual and asked if I had any plans later that night. Although such a question was strange, I confirmed with him that I had no plans—I would be home all night. That was it. Dinner was had, the boys were put to bed and our feet were up. Suddenly, a knock on the door—just like last time. Tim answered the door and I heard Mum say 'Is she here?'. Oh no—Mum had that same look of defeat. She confirmed my nightmare. The cancer was back. This time, there were no options. Chemotherapy might prolong her life but that was the only hope. I was to accept that she might have three months to live. I was devastated! It turns out that Mum had spoken to Tim earlier that day to make sure that he would be home to comfort me when she delivered the news. She wanted me to be supported—typical of her selfless attitude.

How was this happening to us again? The cancer had gone—we had just had a scare. I'd learnt the lesson—I was grateful to have my mum. I made cups of tea and we sat and chatted about the chemotherapy. I let her make the decision. It wasn't mine to make. She was terrified of the horrible poison and decided not to go through with it. I stood by her choice. I understood her reasons. I wanted time with my mum but I wasn't in any position to tell her what to do.

After many shared tears, I jumped in the car with her and we set off on a two hour drive to deliver the news once again to her brothers and sister. The whole way we talked and cried. We spoke of her not seeing my boys—her grandsons—grow. We spoke of all of the milestones she was going to miss. We spoke of our own life events that we would now not be able to share. We cried and cried and had to keep swapping who drove for fear of an accident! We were welcomed by my aunty on that cold night and propped in front of the wood heater with strong hot coffee.

Mum, my aunty and I sat together in a circle of disbelief. Mum explained that she was not interested in chemotherapy this time so we discussed alternative therapies. After a few hours of talking and many more tears, it was time to make our long way back home as it was very late. We slumped back into Mum's car—both of us utterly exhausted—and set off home.

On our drive, I told my mum that I could not imagine her missing from my life. She confirmed that she didn't want to miss out on watching my boys grow and witness me mature. We had often giggled about the boys and their future experiences at school or sports. All of these potential moments were being threatened. It was too hard to comprehend. Basically, I chose to take that path—to not comprehend. Then it didn't have to feel real! I sat in the car staring out into the darkness with an overwhelming feeling of fear consuming me. I was not sure what to do to make the situation easier for Mum. I just wished that it was all a nightmare and that I was going to wake up. I cried myself to sleep that night.

On reflection, not once did I hear Mum say 'Why me?'. In fact, once I asked her how she could be so accepting and she said, 'Why not me?'.

2 May 2006

Today I went out and got a tattoo. I LOVE it. I have been working on a design for a little while and these past few days I have felt very strongly that the time is right to get it done. So today was the day—no looking back—and I'm positive that I will never regret this permanent reminder of my adoration for my mum. My tattoo is a Kanji symbol on my left shoulder that says 'Mother' and underneath it reads 'courage' and 'love'. I had this done in honour of Mum—both because of her being my beloved mother and because she has proven to be the strongest woman I have ever known. Mum is so stoic and yet always full of love. This defines what a mother is in my opinion. To be able to love and fiercely live is simply inspiring. The tattooist asked me if anyone would storm into his shop and punch him for doing it. I reassured him that this would definitely not happen. This experience has been so satisfying for me. Mum, herself, wasn't thrilled as she thinks that I am going to end up covering myself in tattoos—I only have two currently—but this tattoo means the world to me. Secretly, I think she liked it a tiny little bit!

14 May 2006

It's Mother's Day today. Mum came over for a nice big breakfast and I spoiled her rotten! Now, I'm left sitting here thinking of next year's Mother's Day. How will it feel if Mum is gone? How will I get through the day without feeling angry or absolutely devastated? Every Mother's Day in my entire life has involved my mum! Thinking about the day without her now makes me feel sick. It would be so great to get another 20 years of her life. Such a small ask in so many ways. So many people don't even have to consider it—some don't even value it—I could vomit...

The realisation that I could lose Mum consumed me. I tried so hard to be a present mother for my boys, but I was petrified every waking minute of every day. I tried not to think about the harsh outcome of Mum's disease too often but, when I did, it was just far too devastating to comprehend. I was consumed with sadness.

26 May 2006

The strangest thing happened to me today. I was walking at the shops and my eyesight just went. All I could see was black. I was pushing Kye in the pram and felt so scared that I couldn't see anything. I then got a tiny bit of sight back so looked for a chair to sit on and rest. My heart was thumping. I felt like I was going to die! I was sitting next to a lady and asked her if my eyes looked strange. I could barely see her. She just shrugged. I don't think she was interested in having a conversation with me at all. Thankfully Kye was well behaved so I just sat until I could see again. All I could think was that I should get my eyes looked at so I found an optometrist. I felt so silly telling them about my experience but they suggested that it sounded like a panic attack. I've never had one before but man it freaked me out! Time to see my GP I think. So scary!

The pressure was becoming unbearable and impacting my day-to-day life. I was stuck in a nightmare that I could not escape. No matter how hard I tried to be positive, I just couldn't keep it up. My world was crashing.

12 June 2006

I'm not having a very good day today. Someone suggested that I should start taking some antidepressants. I feel so uninspired and really don't want to do anything. I'm having so many ups and downs. I must be so horrible and unpredictable to be around. The weather is lousy and that never helps, but also the sad reality of Mum's illness is torturing me. I feel as though I am trapped and suffocating and nothing I do will ease the pain for me. I'm so scared. I think I need to make an appointment with the doctor.

*I spoke to Mum after her oncology appointment today and it is not good news. The doctor examined her liver area and told her that he could tell the tumour was growing. He mentioned that chemo could still be an option. She doesn't want chemotherapy or radiology. I don't blame her. She wants quality of life and is so scared of what strong medication will do to her. It must be such a hard decision to make. She does not want to leave everyone but also doesn't want to put herself through the pain and horror of chemotherapy. It's a rotten situation that just won't go away! If only I could just take it away from her. I sat in the lounge this evening listening to Coldplay's 'Fix You' over and over and over. I just cried and cried. I'm so sick with sadness...*

Although the circumstances were not good, it was nice to have my mum home again. The boys and I would spend almost every day at her house making memories and appreciating the quality time together. Every now and then I would be forced to acknowledge the illness, as Mum would feel nauseous or experience some pain. Mostly, though, she was just my normal Mum and my boys' Nanny and we were having a nice time. I tried not to think about the reality of losing her in my life. It was a thought that I couldn't bare. I became conditioned to bury certain emotions. I knew that I would have to face them all one day—just not yet. Already, I was noticing other daughters and their mothers together. They didn't seem to have a care in the world. I envied them. I wanted so badly to stop them and question if they truly appreciated each other—to ask them if they knew how lucky they were. The lessons were beginning. Gratitude was slowly becoming a part of my daily existence.

My brother and his family came from Japan to stay with Mum for a while. This would be their precious time together with her before she died. It was one of the best times in my adult life so far, having so many of my family members together. A dark cloud loomed though. It was not going to have a happy outcome, but being together was all we could do and for that time it was nice.

After much thought, Mum decided to take on a course of chemotherapy. She opted for something quite strong with the hope that it would decrease the size of the tumour in her liver and give her some more time. Time was all she wanted. She would have bought it if she could. The thought of missing out on seeing my brother and I become middle-aged, our children start school and grow into men—it was too much for her to accept. I know she was almost as frightened of the side effects of chemo as she was of dying, but I guess she felt that it was worth a try. After all, what did she have to lose?

I was ready and on standby to attend to anything Mum needed as she embarked on a hideous couple of months. Again, her treatment was one week on then two weeks off. It was so hard to stand by and witness the destruction that is chemotherapy. There was not much I could do for Mum and she was very independent, never wanting to bother anyone. She rarely asked for anything. I cleaned her home, made meals to keep in her freezer, did her washing and shopping, collected her medicine—all those jobs that saved her precious time and energy. At the very least, I allowed Mum to rest and nourish herself when she was interested in eating. Thankfully, the chemotherapy sessions yielded positive results on her tumour and it shrunk substantially. While the tumour didn't disappear, in our opinion, the hideous experience bought her some time. Thank God. For that, we were thankful.

6 September 2006

I feel as though I am in a constant state of panic at the moment. I just can't catch my breath lately. Life is so tough at times and I just want to feel normal. I want to spend time with my family and just laugh. I want to enjoy days out and be carefree. I want to not feel guilty and not have a heavy sadness crushing my heart. I don't understand how it all works. Mum loves her life but it's threatened. I've lost faith in the system of life. I'm behaving terribly to Tim. I'm just sick of it all. I'm crabby towards the kids and I'm not happy with myself at all! I feel as though I just walk around yelling at everyone and I'm the worst mother ever. I have no self-esteem and I'm worried that my kids will grow up like me. Unfortunately I'm the one they spend 98 per cent of their time with, poor things. I'm my own worst enemy. I just want to be happy!

Life for Tim, the kids and myself was certainly rough. There was not much to celebrate but we knew that we had to do something to make us happy. Otherwise things would just get worse.

We made a major decision to relocate to a beautiful part of the Victorian coastline. This was something we had talked about for years but there always seemed to be a reason that stopped us going. I was hesitant about leaving Mum but it was only a one-hour drive away and I knew she would be ok. The time was right for us. We needed this sea change and it was where our hearts belonged. We began to improve our home for a better sale price.

Mum was feeling well and decided to carry on with life as though all was normal. She craved normality and began to plan things. She painted walls in her house, arranged to update her bathrooms and kitchen and bought new furniture. I guess she felt the need to turn over a new leaf. She hadn't cured the cancer but she did put in a damn good fight. For now, she had slowed cancer down and this was worth celebrating.

Travel was always a major goal of Mum's. So far, in her adult life, she had been to Japan, Vietnam, China (about six times), Vienna, Germany, Greece, Italy and all over Australia. She was so inspiring to me. Next on her travel list—if her oncologist approved it—were England and France. And I was invited.

# Chapter 4

13 September 2006

Well, I was feeling that I needed an adventure and now I've got one. Mum and I are going to England and France! She got the clearance from her oncologist. I'm so excited! It all feels surreal. I'll be leaving my three young boys and jetting off with my beautiful mum. Tim is going to take time off to be with the kids. I can't believe it! Leigh Van Der Horst—exhausted and overworked mother of three lively little boys—is going overseas! AMAZING.

I was about to embark on a trip with my mum that would begin a huge change in me—I just didn't realise it yet. The logistics of organising for me to be out of the family mould for almost 20 days were huge. I didn't have long to get organised—but there was so much to do. I had to: update my passport; arrange some childcare so Tim could get some work done; and make some meals to freeze so my family didn't live on beans on toast or takeaways for the next few weeks. I knew how busy Tim would be while I was away. He was going to finish off our renovations and have our home photographed and on the market before I got back. Not once did he put any pressure on me or make me feel bad for upping and leaving. He knew how important this trip was to Mum and I. Bless him.

*16 October 2006*

*I AM IN LONDON! I can't believe it. Man, the plane ride was rough! I shed a tear when we landed. Silly, but I think the realisation of just how far away I am from my boys hit me. I feel sick in my stomach, both from fear of the distance between my boys and I and hoping like crazy that Mum can enjoy this wonderful experience with no complications. I'm excited though. I never thought I would be doing this at this stage of my life. I am sitting in bed in our little hotel room situated right in the heart of Trafalgar Square. Its 6:15pm and I am struggling to stay awake. I'm planning to sleep like a log! I should— if the sirens don't keep me awake. A constant stream of police sirens can be heard. It's nuts! Anyway, we have lots planned so I have to catch up on some sleep. I'm so grateful for this once-in-a-lifetime opportunity.*

Mum and I wasted no time in playing tourist. We set out early on our first day and walked over the Millennium Bridge to sit next to the London Eye where we sipped hot coffee. To just sit together with Mum with the beautiful sunshine on my back—so far from my normal life— was so surreal. I almost had to pinch myself! We jumped on a bus tour that took us all over London, taking note of places that we wanted to visit on foot. I was beaming! Nothing could wipe the smile off my face and Mum was the same. We must have looked like two crazy ladies who had never seen buses and buildings before. Every corner we turned was another postcard-worthy sight. We were only hours into the trip and I had already nearly filled the memory card on my camera. Everything was just beautiful!

As well as spotting famous landmarks, I was secretly hoping to spy Chris Martin from Coldplay. Thankfully I had Mum to bring me back to earth and tell me not to be so silly. Well, I thought there might at least have been a slim chance.

Our huge day ended at Trafalgar Square—all beautifully lit up—where we sipped hot chocolates and watched people going by. We'd had a huge day of chatting and walking. We were both exhilarated but exhausted—and it was only our first day! I knew this holiday was going to be something really special.

20 October 2006

We have been so busy! So far, we have toured Oxford, Stratford-upon-Avon and Warrick Castle. I've taken a million photos. We have wandered the streets of London and done some shopping. We even visited Harrods, which was unbelievable. I loved the elaborate décor—but I did wonder how you would get out in a hurry if there was a fire. Harrods seemed very closed in! I'm missing my boys but enjoying every minute of this experience.

Mum is like a walking history book. No need for a tour guide when I am with her. She's full of knowledge, so intelligent. What would I do without her? Must sleep now.

21 October 2006

Mum and I went to Notting Hill today. We had a look around the Portobello Market. It was very cool! At one point, it started to pour with rain. Wow, it really buckets down here. We took cover in shops and browsed the racks of clothes. I bought a few things but Mum didn't bother. It's sad that Mum has no interest in buying anything for herself. Maybe she wonders what the point would be? She was talking today about not living beyond January or February. She is annoyed, as she loves her life but was so unhappy years ago and now wishes to have more time. I said to her, 'Lessons are meant to be learned from life. I'm not sure what this lesson is'. She replied, 'The lesson is to appreciate and enjoy each day'. Yep—well said.

24 October 2006

We have done so much over the past few days. My head touches the pillow each night and I'm off like a light. Mum and I have been to Paris and toured the Eiffel Tower, The River Sienne and the Louvre. What a beautiful city. I would love to go back one day with Tim and explore the Parisian streets a little more.

While sipping lattes at a very chic café the other day, we were referred to as a 'lovely couple'. We have never giggled so much in our lives. Mum took it as such a compliment being mistaken for my girlfriend, as I am so much younger. I assured her that clearly I was a gold digger and liked much older women. Oh we laughed! Can you just imagine?

Once we got back to London, we arranged a visit to Stonehenge and Bath on a bus tour. Our tour guide was definitely an interesting lady. She yelled at us all if we talked loudly as she felt it was rude to talk on the bus, even if she wasn't speaking! At one point she told a man off for coughing, saying that he was rude for interrupting. Mum offered him a lozenge as he was almost chocking, the poor guy. At times, Mum and I would have tears streaming down our faces from laughing so hard at the demands this tour guide inflicted on us. To make it worse, she repeated all of her speeches in Japanese—really bad Japanese! She also mentioned that there was a tin at the front of the bus for donations, as she was on very little earnings and would appreciate more money for her efforts. Mum—under her breath—said that she could jam it. This made me first giggle, then cower from the tour guide's subsequent death stare. Now that was a long day!

I sobbed last night when I was in bed. I think that—because I am spending so much time with Mum—the reality of what is going to happen is too hard to grasp. I really have to focus on the here and now. It's hard—but I will try with all of my soul!

25 October 2006

I got a reply email from Tim today telling me to get my act together and enjoy this experience, as I will never have it again. He's right. I sometimes think that I have to make everything perfect and often that is impossible. There really is no way of knowing when cancer will take Mum and I'm not going to dwell on it! That's wasting precious time.

Today, Mum and I did our own thing. I wandered around Camden Market and spent the beautiful sunny afternoon lying on the grass at Regents Park reflecting. I sent Tim a text, telling him how much I loved him. He texted straight back saying that he couldn't sleep as he was thinking about what exciting things I was doing. He's so far away—I really miss him.

28 October 2006

Mum and I have toured the Tower of London, seen Buckingham Palace, Hampton Court Palace, St Paul's Cathedral, Westminster Abbey and tomorrow we are going on the London Eye. Frankly, I'm all toured out! I feel so bad for saying it but I don't think I could physically visit any more attractions. I've had such an amazing holiday. I have enjoyed the time with Mum so much, but it's also been tough to watch her deteriorate each day. I think all the walking has really tired her. Plus, over the past week, her stomach has begun to swell due to a fluid build-up which I know is causing her some pain. Stupid cancer!

I know Mum is looking forward to going home. I think she needs some time to rest and she's a bit anxious about her stomach. She is beginning to feel a bit afraid. I hate that bloody cancer is tainting this trip.

30 October 2006

We are leaving tomorrow. I've had a wonderful holiday and learnt so much, but Mum is in a really bad way. Her stomach has swollen a lot and she is nervous about the flight. Hopefully it is just fluid and she will be able to have it drained out when she gets home. I'm reassuring her that everything will be OK and I won't leave her side. We are spending a night in Singapore, which should help as it will give her a chance to rest.

31 October 2006.

We are in beautiful Singapore. I'm at the pool while Mum is resting in our room. I begged her to come and join me, as the weightlessness she would feel in the water would really ease her pain—but she can't fit into her bathers anymore. I feel so sad for her. She is in quite a lot of pain and I know she doesn't have enough medication on her to ease it. As we left Heathrow, there was an issue with our stop-over. We were told that our bags would continue on and we would collect them later in Melbourne. No-one had informed us of this, so I lost my shit and demanded that we be able to access them as Mum had to have her medication. I shocked myself a bit with my abrupt reaction, but I really just wanted Mum to have her stuff and not have to worry. That's the least she deserves. I think the staff at Heathrow got all of my fears and frustrations thrown at them. Anyway, we have our bags! Leaving early tomorrow and home to my boys tomorrow night. I miss them so much that my heart hurts...

The final flight home was tough. Mum was really uncomfortable and in a great deal of pain. She ate nothing and coped as best as she could. It was so challenging to keep her comfortable in the tiny economy seats. If I were rich I would have demanded first class for her! At one stage, she was next to an extremely overweight woman who had a slight body odour issue. I offered to swap seats with Mum but she refused. I guess she didn't want to make a fuss. The plane was completely full and Mum just took it all in her stride—she never complained once. I was so in awe of her strength and tenacity. Even when she was scared, in pain and feeling nauseous, she didn't want to make a scene. Unbelievable.

When we landed on our home soil, I hurried ahead to collect our bags so she would not have to wait. She was not in a good state at all. I drove us home and made sure she was safely inside before heading home myself. It was the middle of the night. I crept inside, marvelled at the 'welcome home' sign my boys had made and went to join Tim in bed. What I found was Tim and our three little boys all tucked up together—there was no room at all for me! I snuck off and slept in one of the boys' beds. I was home. It was nice but I couldn't rest. I was worried about Mum—again.

BREATHE

# Chapter 5

It was business as usual not long after arriving home. Our first family home was officially up for sale so life was frantic. I was attempting to keep the house neat with three boys aged six, three and 22 months. What is more, our home was expected to be ready for inspections at any given time—and so was I. For every viewing, I had to disappear with the boys to allow groups of people to look through my home with a fine-toothed comb. Then I had to hear their criticism regarding the choices we had made with our renovations. I didn't take any of it to heart though. After all, I had bigger things going on!

On the advice of her oncologist, Mum went to have fluid drained from her stomach. It was actually amazing to watch. They literally inserted a tube into her stomach and allowed the contents to drain into a bag. She would often end up having up to two or three litres drained at a time.

After this particular procedure, Mum had a scan to take a look at the tumour and its status. The scan revealed that she had developed a new mass of tumours and—if these were left untreated—they would grow so large as to press on her bowel and bladder, eventually causing her to become incontinent. This was a hideous thought for my fiercely independent mother! Again, chemotherapy was recommended and Mum agreed to it. Mostly because there was hope to shrink these tumours and allow her some more time, comfort and dignity.

12 November 2006

Mum is going to start a new round of chemo. I'm glad as this will make her more comfortable and hopefully slow the cancer down. I feel so bad for her as she has been told to expect two to three good months before she becomes very ill. We are all being strong. We are determined to enjoy the good days ahead and support Mum through the bad ones. I'm amazed at my own strength. I'm feeling strong and positive—I have to be this way to deal with everything that is going on around me. Yesterday, I put the boys in the car after doing the shopping and saw the sun was shining. So I stopped for a moment, looked around and thought to my-self—I'm so lucky. Imagine that! With everything that is going on, I am learning to appreciate what I have—such an important tool in life. I told Mum and she agreed whole-heartedly. She said, 'Life's good, Leigh. Life is what you make it!'. Mum has taught me these skills—something I will be forever grateful for…

23 November 2006

This morning I rang Mum to ask if she could baby-sit the boys for a couple of hours today. She said she couldn't as she was having a meeting with the funeral guy to make sure that everything was planned and clear. I know she is doing this to take the weight off my shoulders. I didn't know what to say. I felt like I was going to vomit. People keep asking me how I am. I force a smile and say, 'Oh, I'm fine'. I can feel within myself that I'm not though. My tummy just churns, my appetite is gone and I try to stay so busy that I can't stop and think. I don't want to think—my reality is too sad...

After an unsuccessful auction, we sold our house to a lovely couple. We didn't get as much money as we had hoped for, but we got enough to pay off our family car and walk away with a future deposit for another home. Our next destination was yet to be decided as Mum's deteriorating health was hanging over me like a dark cloud. Every day was a torment. On one hand, I desperately wanted happiness for my little family. We deserved to create a life for ourselves. A life that we had been dreaming of for years. But Mum deserved our attention too. I knew all too well that her time would come to an end and I could hold off on my dreams to offer her the support that she needed. I also wanted to give her all the time that she had to spend with my boys. We had hit a fork in the road. I had to make a decision that was best for everyone.

24 December 2006

It's Christmas Eve. If this is going to be Mum's last Christmas I hope everyone has an enjoyable day! Mum was upset yesterday. She is worried about how Jack will handle all of the sadness once she is gone and she wanted to make sure that I knew how to deal with his emotions. She pointed out that we would have to give him tonnes of love and be extremely patient with him as he could really go off the rails. She had such panic in her voice. It has really shocked me! Mum said that she feels she is letting him down. My poor mum. None of this is fair. On a positive note, the chemotherapy is shrinking the tumour in Mum's stomach and she is feeling more comfortable. I'm grateful for that. Hopefully she has a great day tomorrow.

26 December 2006

I feel as though I am a ticking time bomb at the moment. I know that Mum will die—sooner rather than later—and I HATE knowing that. I have no idea of what I am meant to do with myself until then—whenever that will be. I hate that I am going to lose Mum and I feel a fire burning inside of me that is the uncertainty of my future. I'm reflecting over what was Christmas Day. It's not fair that I might never share another one with her. She enjoyed herself but I caught her a few times just gazing into space. I'm positive that she too was thinking about how unfair it all is. We've decided to live with Mum indefinitely. There is no way of knowing how long this arrangement will work for but, for now, it feels right. I need her as much as she needs me. If only I could find a way to end this horrible nightmare and stop her from dying...

30 January 2007

I saw my doctor today about my moods. He said that he thinks I am doing OK, considering. He reminded me that I have three young children and that that alone can be enough stress to handle at times. I guess he is right. But it doesn't help when you are fearful of your mother dying too. I mentioned to him that I just feel helpless and I can't plan anything for fear of the outcome. He advised me to just make plans one week at a time so I feel a sense of control over 'my' world. We talked about what I can expect to see when Mum deteriorates and what I have to face towards the end. I may not be able to care for her as I hope *to. I can't comprehend that. I will care for her—I have to!*

Although I had made the decision to live with Mum, I couldn't make decisions about anything else. I was just flailing about as a mother to my boys and a wife to my wonderfully patient husband. I was forgetting everything! My mind was so scattered. I felt as though I was on a sickly ride that just kept spiralling and I had no way of getting off. The outcome was going to be dreadful and all I could do was hang on as best as I could.

All the time, well-meaning people would ask how Mum was and I was so tired of repeating the sad news over and over. Still they were trying to convince me that she was going to be all right. I learned that this was their way of coping. Saying the alternative was not possible to them—or kind to me. I would just nod and smile. Not once though, did I believe them. Call me practical, call me glum, but in some way—deep down—I had to be prepared for the worst.

*10 March 2007*

*I feel like I am developing real anger issues. I'm stuck in this horrible dream and I cant escape! My house is so loud and messy all the time and I'm desperate for some quiet to try to process everything that is going on. I'm scared that I am becoming depressed. The boys are always calling out for more and I honestly feel like I don't have any more to give. I'm so tired! I wish I were calmer. I know that I need to slow down and hug more, kiss more, sit more—just 'be' with my boys more. But my mind races and I feel like I can't keep up! Sometimes I seriously feel like I can't breathe. The problem is, I think the boys are feeding off my nervous energy and that's why they are acting out lately. I wish I could just laugh with them but my heart is breaking. I wish I could tell them that my Mum is dying* and they need to look after ME! I wish I could ask Mum for advice but I don't want to worry her. Oh—what to do?

21 March 2007

Well, in three days we will be moving out of our family home and in with Mum for a while. My head is a bit muddled. I'm excited to be staying with Mum and helping her out but sad to close the door on our first home. I know that the future holds lots to be excited about but I have a giant hill to climb right now and I don't know when I'll reach the top. My life is on hold. It's all about Mum now. She is my main focus.

28 March 2007

We have settled into Mum's house well. It's a bit manic but, all in all, everyone is comfortable. Jack is not having bad dreams anymore, which is nice. He must feel safe. I'm wondering where to from here but, for now, this is my focus and I should try not to plan too far ahead. It's just more torture for me to endure.

While settling into life at my mum's house, we received sad news that one of our oldest and dearest friends, Darryl, had developed cancer. His outlook was not good as the cancer was very aggressive. It was confirmed to be in his brain, liver and bones. This news was a total shock to everyone, including him. He was so young. He was our age. Tim and I could not imagine having to face death at our stage of life. This realisation brought a whole new round of feelings within me. It was really hitting me hard that life was fragile and not something to take for granted, even in these hard times. Almost as if to rub salt in our wounded souls, on that same day, a scan revealed that Mum's tumour had grown to the size of a 20 week baby. This was of grave concern as, only weeks prior, it was very small. CRAP! Plans were quickly underway for Mum to undergo more treatment, which we hoped would buy her more time.

Mum's cancer was a permanent black cloud that just loomed heavily over all of us. Sometimes it lifted slightly, but not for long. I just couldn't understand the cruelty in life. Sadly, some things can never be explained.

28 July 2007

I'm so scattered at the moment. Tim and I are not getting along very well, most likely due to my mood swings. Sometimes I just wish I could sleep all day long and forget about all the crap that is happening. I feel like my soul is broken. I have nothing to give. I can't be bothered relating to anyone anymore. I can't laugh. It actually hurts to smile. I'm always saying no to coffee invites. I'm hurting. Nothing feels good. There is nothing driving me. I wish that I could just look into a crystal ball and see what is to come...

19 August 2007

I'm so sick of being me! I'm forever searching for ways to make myself feel happy and complete—and I am starting to wonder if that will EVER happen. I'm so low. I just don't know what to do. I feel like I need something to motivate me—some hope. I feel as though I have no sense of self, no purpose and nothing to give. I know I have to snap out of this way of thinking—I just don't know how. We are moving to the beach in four to five weeks. It became a decision made out of desperation. Our happiness will depend on it! It's the right thing for us to do as a family. I feel extreme guilt, but we all agree it has to happen now. We need a fresh start and Mum has promised to come and stay. I'm looking forward to the sea change but just hope the timing is OK...

I was slowly beginning to understand that life was precious and to be valued. Not only was Mum fighting for her life. Tim and I were also now witnessing our dear friend, who was as young as us, hanging on tight to his much-wanted existence. Up until then, it hadn't really occurred to me that life could be taken from anyone at any time—no matter what their age. I was very grateful for my life, but scared and confused too. What if something were to happen to Tim? Or to me? Or to our boys? There was far too much at risk. I almost felt guilty that I had everything I ever wanted. I felt as though it might be taken away from me. I realised that I had to be grateful for every single thing in my life—no matter what.

# Chapter 6

Our move to the beach was a refreshing change for us all. As each day went by, I became more comfortable with the choice that we had made. Being such a worrier, however, I just could not stop thinking about Mum. I felt like I had let her down. I was constantly on the phone to her and she kept insisting that she was fine. I did fear not having any friends in my new hometown. But I also had faith that, in time, all of that would naturally fall into place.

There was such healing in my new surrounds. I really benefited from time at the beach, just listening to the waves crash and strolling along the sandy shore. It felt like I was *finally home.*

21 September 2007

It has taken me a while to settle into our new surroundings but it feels right. As a family, we have enjoyed long walks along the beach just chatting and being together. Life by the sea feels so much calmer. There is not as much rushing around as I am used to and—to be honest—I love the slow pace. The locals are lovely and welcoming, the scenery is amazing and the boys are already planning all of the adventures they hope to have come summer. This move has definitely been a good choice. Mum is excited for us and insists that if we are happy, then so is she. I hope so.

4 October 2007

Someone said to me recently, 'Your Mum's illness is not yours to take on board. Her sadness is hers to own. You can't absorb it all'. They were right. I can't control any of the crap that Mum is going through. She knows I'm devastated. She knows that I'll do anything in the world for her. She knows that I love her to the moon and back. But she would never want me to carry the emotion and fear that she carries. Just as I wouldn't if it were my own kids and I in this position. I have to try and lighten my emotional load for the sake of Tim and the boys. Jack seems happier and is doing well at his new school, thank goodness. We are all smiles, which is a nice change.

15 October 2007

My 32nd birthday.

Will this be my last birthday with Mum in my life? I hope not. That thought has consumed me all day. It's not a nice feeling. Mum gave me a card with a beautiful painting of the beach on the front and inside she wrote, 'This is my wish for you. May there always be sand, sunshine and happiness'. I cried. We spent the day taking in the stunning sights at my local beaches. She was in awe and so happy for us. I am so grateful that she has had the chance to experience our new life and all that it offers.

26 November 2007

Life feels strangely but happily sweet at the moment. We have had a lot of fun and social gatherings. The kids are really happy and the Christmas buzz is in the air. I love this time of year. My Christmas cards are all done and ready to go out in the first week of December. I'm also collecting decorations to put up around the house in readiness for our annual Christmas Party this coming weekend. I love that there are gifts lying around the house— giving really does feel good. I'm so thrilled that Mum is going to spend Christmas with us. She has not had a big Christmas in years. I do wonder, though, if this will be her last. I wonder that every time a big event takes place. I just don't dwell on the thought— its too sad. I choose instead to make the most of every moment.

25 December 2007

I'm exhausted! It's evening on Christmas Day and the day has been so full on. We woke with Mum and exchanged gifts, which was the best. I loved having her here and— although at times she became very tired—she soldiered on and really enjoyed her day. At times it was very loud, which can be a bit too much for Mum, but she did well. I'm so glad to have spent Christmas Day with her. Darryl also came and spent some time with us in celebrating the big day. The poor boy does not look good at all. He knows this is his last Christmas. That must be so hard to face, but he doesn't burden anyone. He is such an amazing guy. He told Tim that he was ready to let go. It breaks my heart.

I felt some sort of sudden awakening that festive time of year. All around were celebrations and happiness, but we were more than aware of the sadness and impending death that were knocking on Darryl's door—and soon enough, Mum's too. It was very strange to be celebrating joyful events while those close to us were dying. I began to see everything in a different light though. I was so grateful for every day. I was healthy, my family was healthy and we were living our dream life by the water. I was so thankful for everything that I had—yet I knew nothing in life was guaranteed.

24 January 2008

Summer is well and truly keeping us busy. I feel happy and fulfilled with my life, which is a welcome feeling. We have been catching up with friends, both old and new, plus spending long days out on the boat snorkelling and swimming. One day, we found a beautiful private spot and just stayed there for the whole day. The boys bobbed up and down with their life jackets on. This gave me the chance to just sit quietly, reflect and remind myself of just how wonderful my life is. With everything going on around us, we are very lucky to live the life we do.

Each time I see Mum, I notice that the tumour in her stomach is getting bigger. She is happy though and remains positive and independent. She is teaching me so much about appreciating what I have and making the best of everything. She is such a strong, amazing woman and I'm so thankful that she is my mum!

Life was a constant flow of peaks and troughs for us. We loved what we had created for our little family and especially adored the laughter that oozed naturally from our boys. But we were often brought crashing down to earth when thinking about our loved ones who were unwell. Most days either Tim or I would visit Darryl as his health was rapidly declining, which was a very frightening prospect. He became more heavily medicated each time we saw him, as his pain was at an unbearable level.

It was so intense to sit back and watch this happen to a special friend who we loved so dearly. He knew that he didn't have long to live and—although he would have given anything to be well and live out his life—a part of him was at peace. Each day I would get strange shivers running up my spine and would wonder if he'd passed away. It was a torturous time. Tim spent most of his waking hours with Darryl. His heart was breaking. All I could do was make sure that I was there for Tim when he needed me and yet I still worried constantly about my mother. Life was definitely bittersweet.

7 February 2008

We lost beautiful Daz today. Tim was one of the privileged ones to be with him when he died. It will shake him up for a while. It's strange when someone you love dies. The uncertainty of where they are now. It's just so final. I'm going to miss Darryl. He fought so graciously. The only comfort I feel is that he is no longer in pain. I will love him forever in my heart.

24 March 2008

The past month has been a haze of grief. I have barely had the energy to journal. We all really miss Darryl and I, personally, feel a sense of guilt that I have my life and continue to live on. I know that sounds silly, but he was just too young and had so much to live for. Darryl was newly married and he should have had the chance to be a father. Life is so very precious, it really is.

I saw Mum today. Her rapid weight loss really shocked me. It's only been a week since I saw her last and she has lost so much weight in that time. Her face, particularly, is looking extremely thin, which makes her eyes seem huge. Her skin is so pale. It's scary how fast this is happening. I've processed the idea of losing her—as much as I possibly can—and that is a devastating thought. But it's the journey to that point that scares me the most. I wonder what the date will be when Mum leaves this life? I wish I could somehow prepare myself for all of this. The road ahead is going to be very scary...

# Chapter 7

The end for my beautiful mother was drawing closer. It had been a long, exhausting journey with so many ups and downs. But now, just looking at Mum was confirmation that her time was running out. It tortured me to see her so thin. She still smiled her big, wide smile and her beautiful hazel eyes still sparkled, but the rest of her body was failing her at such a rapid rate. It hurt me inside to witness this, but I felt strong. I was scared, but I was also prepared and ready to be her rock.

I focused on the fact that, right then and there, nothing else mattered. I had a single goal: to guide my mother to reach the end of her life with dignity and without pain. I believe that she had worked some magic on me over the past few years to help me reach that point and be the solid support that she so desperately needed.

6 May 2008

I'm spending a couple of days at Mum's. She is not good. She is so thin and yesterday morning, while we were talking about her illness, she became really upset. Mum said that she hates that she will miss out on the boys' lives. She feels that this is not fair and not what she wants. Then she apologised for the emotional vent—typical of my mum.

Afterwards, we hugged and I just rubbed her bony back. My fingers rippled along her spine—she has no body fat at all. My poor, beautiful and battered Mum. It's so sad to watch her go through this and mostly go through it alone. Later today, we are going to visit her specialist for an update. I'm dreading it...

9 May 2008

Well, I'm gutted. Mum's cancer has finally taken over her body. Game over—this horrid disease has bloody won. I spoke to Mum's specialist on the phone and he informed me that she has only several weeks to live. He advised me that it's too optimistic to assume that she would still be alive in two months. Instead, he said, Mum is teetering at the top of a really fast, slippery slope.

As Mum's specialist was explaining all this, my heart was pounding out of my chest. The words that I have NEVER wanted to hear were being said and the reality of losing my mother forever was confirmed to be something that would happen soon.

To assume that my beautiful Mum will be dead by June or July is incomprehensible. I have informed all of the family and no-one knows what to do. We all feel so helpless. Jim is coming home in three weeks to stay for a short while, so that gives Mum something positive to focus on. I'm so sad and so scared at the thought of not having a mum. What the hell am I going to do without her? I'm going to miss her so much, I just can't bare the reality of it all! Why is this happening? Why can't someone just bloody fix it?

21 May 2008

My life is so strange at the moment. I am spending lots of time with Mum and I am really grateful to be able to do so without the kids. But I miss my boys. I know that they miss me too and are confused about what is going on.

Mum and I have been sitting quietly, knitting and chatting openly about everything. It's as though there is a ticking clock with us constantly. We know the time will soon run out and we still have so much to say to each other. I sit and absorb Mum's words of wisdom. She told me how amazing she thinks I am and how much she adores Tim and the boys. I told her that I am who I am due to her and her inspiring attitude. I told her that I just can't imagine my life without her, as I need her. Mum responded by telling me that she needs us too.

While Mum sounds well, she doesn't look well. She has no fat anywhere on her body, but her tummy is huge. I just don't know how I am going to handle this. I wish I knew how long she had left. I wish I could keep her alive. I can't imagine not having her around. What is going to happen to me when this is all over? What will I do when she is not here? I dare not think about it…

23 May 2008

Mum has had a craving for tomato soup lately—the really artificial kind from a tin. This is not usually her thing as she eats quite wholesomely as a rule. But tonight, she insisted that I go out and stock up for our dinner.

After my trip to the supermarket, I heated up the soup

and we sat down together to watch a movie that Mum has been desperate to see. Well, I could not think of a more inappropriate movie to be consuming bowls of blood-red tomato soup in front of. In fact, I doubt that I will ever feel the need to eat tomato soup again. Mum's movie choice? 'Sweeney Todd: The Demon Barber of Fleet Street'! Literally two hours worth of splattering blood. It made us laugh so much. Not the movie itself, but the sudden effort it us took to digest our eagerly anticipated tomato soup. I'm pretty sure that Mum dealt with that craving! It was so good to laugh though. I'll miss that...

24 May 2008

Boy I have a short fuse today! I have been at Mum's for the past few days and now I'm back at home—but frankly, I just want to be with Mum. I feel terrible about that, but I want to look after her and make sure that she is OK. I'm so frustrated. I'm constantly in a state of panic—I am a tight knot of anxiety. I just wish I could let go of all the pressure and relax. I don't want any of this anymore. I want to stop this horrible nightmare.

Every day, when I wake up, the first thing I wonder is whether today will be the day. I have no idea what to expect. I dread the first round of anniversaries where Mum won't be here. I'm so scared...

28 May 2008

Today is Mum's 56th birthday. It has been very un-eventful. I gave Mum a gift that she loved and we were going to go out for lunch, but she was not well enough. She sat all morning—barely moving due to nausea—showered at 1pm and then just sat again, feeling really sick. I said that we didn't have to go out if she didn't want to and she quickly agreed. Mum then went back to bed and woke at 5:30pm. She had a very light tea before returning straight to bed. It was nice to see her light up when Jim rang though. She was so happy to hear from him. I sat outside her door, listening to the sound of joy in her voice. It's a sound that is becoming more rare now. My heart literally hurts. I wish I had some magical power to take it all away. This, I know, is the last time that I'll spend her birthday with her. My throat is just so sore from emotion—it's all just sitting there, waiting to explode out of me.

29 May 2008

I crashed Mum's car today. As if she doesn't have enough to worry about, I messed up her much-loved car! It was so stupid of me. I went out to grab some food for us and as I turned a corner, I just drove straight into the back of another car. Clearly my head is elsewhere. Thankfully, the lady in the other car was really nice and I just bawled my eyes out. She asked if I was OK and I quickly explained that this is my Mum's car, that she is unwell and that I am just so sad. She gave me a big hug and rubbed my back until I calmed down, bless her. Unfortunately, I did damage both of our cars so I have to deal with it all through insurance. This is just another headache that we don't need. When I came home and told Mum, she surprised me. Instead of being angry, which I was expecting, she just hugged me tight and assured me that it was going to be OK. Then, after sharing some tears, we burst out laughing as I recalled my emotional outburst towards the other driver on a busy main highway! We agreed that I was lucky to have hit someone so caring, but we both felt sorry for her! She got about two years worth of my built-up emotions thrown in her direction. Talk about a big drama!

6 June 2008

I'm staying with Mum again and so is Jim. It's nice—just like the old days, but without Dad of course. Today it was nice to see Mum go out. She stayed in bed all morning but got up slowly to go out with a friend for lunch. She returned by about 4:30pm and then went straight back to bed. The whites of her eyes are beginning to turn yellow and she looks so thin and aged. She mentioned that she didn't sleep well last night as she had to go to the toilet a lot and she felt lots of pain due to the tumours surrounding her liver. Again, I just wish I knew what was going to happen! It's driving me nuts and I'm so scared. Every night that I stay with her I kiss her goodnight, hold onto her tight and wonder if that will be the last kiss—I have no idea. I even sneak up to her room in the morning and peer through the door looking for the rise and fall of her chest. I'm going crazy with fear.

Mum was admitted to hospital on the belief that they would be able to drain four to five litres of fluid from her stomach. It was hoped that this would give her some much-needed comfort. Sadly, though, only two litres were collected as the remaining pressure and swelling was all tumour. A blood test result indicated that she had an extremely low white blood cell count and a transfusion was ordered immediately.

Mum was rather excited about the blood transfusion as she assumed it would give her some much-needed energy and make her feel 'like a million dollars'. She was so selfless and strong—such an amazing woman and role model. That she could be so upbeat at a time when good news was rarely delivered just astounded me. I was in awe of her all the time.

Once Mum was discharged from hospital, I made plans to stay with her for a number of days. Sadly, the transfusion made no difference to her energy levels and she looked no better. She was losing the fight. There were no more solutions. Mum told me that she needed me. I needed her too. It was essential that I had every second I possibly could have in her company. I had to soak it all up as I was well aware that it was coming to an end.

16 June 2008

I keep thinking that one day, after Mum is gone, I am going to look back at all of these journal entries and appreciate the memories that I am recording. In the future, I must remind myself that Mum is so grateful for what I have done. She said tonight that she is so lucky to have me here and that it is a real gift. I told her that I felt the same way.

18 June 2008

I'm so tired, last night I eventually got to sleep at about 2am. My mind was racing. Poor Mum has had a rough day today. She has felt very tired and unwell and has stayed in bed all day. When I give her cuddles, I'm afraid I will break her as she is so bony and fragile. When she lies in bed, she looks so much older than she is. She is just skin and bone. I feel as though I have become so tough that I can't cry. I'm scared of being vulnerable—that if I start to cry, I won't stop! Every so often, a horrible feeling creeps into my throat and I just have to swallow it hard. There is nothing that I can do to change this situation and that's so tough.

Poor Mum's legs are swollen. They look so thick. I have been gently massaging cream into them to relieve some of the pain. My biggest wish for her is that this journey will be as pain-free as possible. I would hate to know that she is suffering. A pain-free process for Mum is all that I can hope for.


22 June 2008

Jim left today.

Last night, Jack and I stayed at Mum's. In the late evening, Jim sat next to Mum in her bed and they talked. I listened to the conversation. Mum was saying that this is not fair and that she is angry that she will miss watching our boys grow up. She started to get upset and said that there is not much that she can't handle but the thought of us suffering after she is gone is more than she can bare.

I became weepy listening to Mum share how she felt and so did Jim. I went to lie down next to Jack but I couldn't get to sleep, I felt so sad, so angry, so utterly devastated. I just lay in bed and sobbed quietly. My heart feels wounded.

In the morning, Jim spent some precious time alone with Mum. Then came the dreaded time that I had to take him to the airport. Just before he left, Jim stood at the bedroom door savouring his final moments with our mum while she lay in her bed. He said, 'Bye Mum, I love you'. Her eyes welled up with tears and she replied, 'Bye love, I love you too'. It was the most heartbreaking moment of my life. Utter torture. Both Jim and Mum know in their hearts that they will never see each other again in this world. I have never felt the kind of pain that I feel right now. I want to turn it off. It just hurts so much.

As I drove Jim to the airport, we were both silent—each of us deep in our own thoughts. We were trying to comprehend what we knew was inevitable—desperately trying to make sense of the impending death of our much loved mother.

Jim felt terrible for leaving, but he had a life in Japan and had taken as much time away as he could to spend with Mum. Now, however, reality demanded that he go back to his daily responsibilities. I assured him that I would keep him up-to-date with everything. We hugged at the departure gate and I walked back to my car with sunglasses on and tears streaming down my face. There was just so much sadness.

# Chapter 8

*26 June 2008*

*Mum stayed in bed until 3:30pm today. She then spent the remaining afternoon and evening lying on the couch. She is exhausted. Mum said that she is so annoyed that her life is being cut short, as she loves it so much. She mentioned that she is not coping with the uncertainty of how long she has left. I suggested that perhaps we should both go and see her specialist for some clear information.*

*I never want Mum to leave. I know no life other than the one with my mother in it. She is an anchor that keeps me firmly grounded and without her around, I'm not sure how I will cope. It's like I am standing back and watching someone else's life. I have no control at all and neither does she. I value my life so much now. I see all the amazing things that surround me and I know that Mum would do anything to keep her own life, also filled with wonderful things. I keep asking myself why this is happening.*

My poor mum. Things around her were becoming so final. One of her best friends cried when she said goodbye to Mum after having afternoon tea out together. Her phone rang almost off the hook with calls from people who were concerned about her – but Mum never bothered to answer it. Then another of her friends called over to say goodbye, as she was heading off travelling for a couple of months and knew that she would never see Mum again. It was all so morbid. I felt so sad for Mum. She was just waiting to die. This wonderful woman— who once was such a socialite and so independent—was now just seeing out her days. It was torture to watch. It must have been such a frightening place for her to be…

30 June 2008

Mum has been admitted into hospital for another transfusion. She also needs some meds to help bring her appetite back up. The doctor has said that if she doesn't take these measures, she will rapidly get worse. Poor Mum, I can't imagine what is going through her mind.

One of the nurses at the hospital said that I am doing a great job with Mum. I'm not doing anything too amazing. I'm the lucky one in all of this. I get to support her through everything while securely knowing that Tim is doing an incredible job at home with our boys. He is providing for them so well and they love having him around.

Tim told me that he feels bad because he won't be there for me when Mum dies as he will be with the boys. I reminded him that he is making this all so much easier by allowing me to spend this time with Mum. I'm so lucky to have such a supportive husband. I know Mum loves him too.

2 July 2008

It's Wednesday today and poor Mum is going to have to stay in hospital until next Monday at this stage. Her specialist is worried that if something happens over the weekend at home, the resources won't be there to cater for her needs. This frightens me so much. Are we getting that close to her death? It makes me feel so ill.

Mum is so thin. Her arms are skin and bone and she has almost no appetite. She tried to have a joke with the nurse today and said that she'd always wanted thin arms. I chuckled but the nurse didn't. Perhaps Mum's comic timing is a little off...

Maybe it won't be long now? I plan to come back and stay with Mum on Monday when she is discharged from hospital. All I hope is that she doesn't suffer...

6 July 2008

Mum called to say that she won't be home until Wednesday at this stage. Her hospital stay just keeps getting longer. She doesn't want to come home yet and I think she is a bit scared. This is the first time that I've sensed her being frightened. I will go back tomorrow—taking some fresh underwear and necessities—to check on her. She is very breathless. Everything is becoming so hard for her.

I would take the boys in to visit Mum while she was in hospital. It was a two and half hour round trip to do this. We would come all set with goodies so I knew that it would be quality time—not just for the boys, but for Mum and I also. I would pack the portable DVD player with Dora and The Wiggles, pencils and colouring books, bags of chips, fruit, sandwiches, lollypops—whatever it took for the boys to sit quietly and behave as a hospital demands. All the same, I had limited time to spend with Mum when I had the boys in tow. Mum understood, but it did make the situation more exhausting for me, that's for sure. Too often, I would be chasing a toddler down the hall at full speed. Not really what I needed, but this was my reality at the time.

7 July 2008

Poor, poor Mum. My heart is breaking. I can't stand to see her in such low spirits and her body is making life so hard for her. I sat with her in hospital for a few hours and just watched her doze. Her dinner came and—after going to the trouble of sitting up—she barely touched it. She needed my help putting her legs up on the bed so she could lie back down. I told her that she could complain in front of me as she is always so accepting and kind. She replied, 'What do I have to complain about?'. She is just so selfless.

Mum's specialist came in and was very honest with her about what is to come. He said that she can stay on at the hospital if she chooses. Mum replied that she doesn't want to go home. They are going to discuss palliative care. I sat there listening to the conversation and just can't believe that this is my reality. This is really happening. I wish I could put a stop to it all. I can't imagine how I will feel once this is all over. Mum doesn't deserve this. It's just not fair.

Mum was admitted into palliative care. She was sharing a room until I demanded that she had her own private room. It took some serious bargaining, but she deserved her privacy. I was not going to give in until I had my own way on this.

Mum's legs became so swollen and she started to get skin tears from the pressure of fluid build-up. This eventually began to leak and caused her quite a lot of pain. The whites of her eyes were really yellow, which

I knew meant a degree of liver failure. I had been warned that she might start to struggle cognitively due to toxins in her blood stream not being processed properly by her failing liver. It was all happening too fast to comprehend.

14 July 2008
It's all just so strange. I don't want to lose my mum EVER but it's going to happen. This is actually happening—and soon. I can't believe it at all!

Mum was so beautiful and kind. While in palliative care, she was waiting for me to come in one day so that I could take some money from her purse and buy one of the cleaners a small gift. She thought perhaps some soap from The Body Shop would be nice. Mum was thankful to this lady, as she had made sure that Mum was delivered a newspaper every morning. I couldn't fathom Mum's selflessness. Here she was, terminally ill, in pain and still thinking of others. What a champion.

I did as she asked. The lady cried and told me that my mum was a beautiful soul, that she and her family were praying for Mum and that what was happening to her was not fair. I nodded, tears welling up.

20 July 2008
I'm taking some time out at Mum's to try and process all of this mess. I'm horrible to the kids and Tim. I do feel so sorry for them but I also feel like a part of me has shut down. I'm so concerned for Mum that I really don't care about much else. I'm so disappointed in the way I am treating the boys though—my beautiful lovely boys. Overall I'm sure it's not that bad, but I'm just not there for them like a mother should be. I know that, in the end, everything will be OK and they really are wonderful little boys.

I went in briefly to see Mum tonight. She is so frail, her skin looks a little darker and her eyes are very yellow. While I was there, she mostly slept. She really can't have much time left.

People keep asking me how I am at the moment and I keep saying that I am OK. It's so easy to say that. It's what Mum says! Like mother, like daughter I suppose. The truth is, though, I'm scared about Mum. Will she be in pain? Will it become embarrassing for her? She's so undeserving of all this. How will it all play out? That is the proverbial million dollar question!

Certain responsibilities at home meant that I could not be with Mum for several days. Although I felt sick to my stomach about this, I had to honour my role as a wife and mum. During this time, I called Mum constantly on the phone but it seemed as though, each time I spoke to her, she was becoming more and more tired. I also noticed that she was becoming shorter of breath and really drowsy. Her days were filled with visitors and often she could not recall who they were. All the same, it was comforting to know that she was not alone.

29 July 2008

I've got the flu. I've been so sick and it is such crappy timing! I've spent the past couple of days at Mum's just resting, as I can barely get out of bed. That means I've been unable to see Mum, which is torture. I dragged myself out this afternoon to visit her. I just had to. She is doing OK but saying odd things. I spoke to the nurses and they agree that Mum is becoming very tired. They also told me that her liver function is getting worse.

I feel so sorry for my beautiful Mum. She lies in her

bed and looks like a little lost girl. Sometimes she looks so confused that it breaks my heart. Other times, she just stares at me and I wonder what she is thinking. I'm scared that she will become more and more confused each time I see her. The nurses said that she might just go into an unconscious state, due to exhaustion. As sad as that would be, it would be best for her. She wants me to take her to the shops tomorrow to buy something. I think she is desperate to feel normal. I'm really nervous about the outing.

30 July 2008

I took Mum to the shops this afternoon. Overall it went well, but man it was hard work emotionally. I kept sweating the whole time because I was anxious—or perhaps it was just the flu talking.

Pushing Mum's wheelchair was hard work and people just stared. It was insane! Often Mum became really confused as to where we were and why. Another reminder of how this outing was very far from normal.

Poor Mum looks so sick. I can barely look at her now without tearing up. We sat in the same food court in which she has burped my babies over the years and I watched as she sipped a Pepsi. I couldn't drink, myself. I felt like I wanted to vomit. I just watched her enjoy the cool fizzy drink as she soaked in the atmosphere. Maybe she knew this was going to be the last time that she experienced what had always been a normal everyday outing for her and for us both together. I took those outings for granted then. Now, knowing that there will be no more of them is all too unbearable.

31 July 2008

I visited Mum this morning and she slept the whole time. Every so often she would say things like, 'I'm not ready yet' or 'I'm not coming'. She would then mutter things about my brother and myself as she dozed. All of this, coupled with her long hours of sleep, was very odd. It was as if she were having a conversation with someone.

The nurse believes that going out yesterday was Mum's last big effort and now she will sleep intensively. I wish she would wake up and chat with me. I would give anything to share a proper talk with her, like we used to do.

1 August 2008

Today Mum was really sleepy and made no sense when she spoke. I hate seeing her this way. It's just not fair. The nurse said that Mum got up this morning and had a shower, but that it made her really tired and she had been asleep since. She advised me to prepare for Mum having only a few days left. Oh my god.

I'm back home now to plan for Jack's 8th birthday tomorrow. I wish that I could be with Mum still. I'm so nervous that she might die without me being there, but Jack needs me too. I rang Mum tonight. I'm not sure that she understood that I was on the phone. I said to my beautiful mum, 'I love you'. She replied, 'I do'.

# Chapter 9

3 August 2008

Today is 3 August 2008 and at 2:10am, my mum died.
Today is the day I have feared for years. Today is the
saddest day of my life.

I feel numb. I am silenced. It hurts to breathe...

I was called into the hospital in the early morning of 2 August 2008—
Jack's 8th birthday. They told me that Mum was deteriorating quickly.
It was the longest drive of my life but, once I got to the palliative
centre, I sat by her side all day. She seemed to be comfortable most of
the time, but would groan every so often. I remained by her side, only
stepping out to visit the toilet. Day became night. Family and friends
would come, say a teary good-bye, give me a sympathetic look and then
hesitantly leave.

Very late in the night, I made the decision to stay at the hospital.
My uncle sat with Mum while I was ushered off into another room
to try and get some rest. I tossed and turned, willing the clock to tick
beyond midnight so that it was not my son's—and her much-loved
grandson's—birthday on which Mum passed.

At about 1am, I woke with a start and realised my gut hurt. It was
churning. I jumped up and rushed across the hall into Mum's room
where she was making unsettling noises—sounds that I will never
forget. Clearly she was in distress. My uncle was trying to calm Mum
down and the nurses gave her some more morphine. Over the next

hour I sat close by Mum's side, stroking her hair and her beautiful hands. I told her how special she was, how much we loved her and how proud we all were of her.

Mum became distressed again and the nurses suggested that we leave the room so they could reposition her and make her more comfortable. They assured me that everything would be OK so, reluctantly, we set off to make a strong cup of tea.

As we made our way up the hall, a nurse came running and calling our names. I could tell by her pace that all was not well. She demanded that we go to Mum immediately. I took a deep breath and then, terrified, I looked at my uncle and ran…

Mum was lying on her left side, so I perched myself on the arm of the recliner chair I had so often sat on while we chatted. I was sitting in a way that made my calves stretch so I could lean over and hold her hand. I was scared to let go—or move for that matter—so I sat like this for close to an hour. I could barely walk for days after due to the pain.

For the first time in hours, I felt Mum's hand clasp mine tightly. The warmth she radiated into me was comforting. Only a mother can provide that soothing bond. I can only imagine that she did not want to go. She would not have wanted to leave me, her daughter. As I sat close by, I told her over and over how wonderful and special she was. I told her how proud we all were of her fight but that now it was time to let go. Time to think of herself and no-one else for a change. I reassured her that Jim and I would be fine, that our children would be fine. It seemed like that right thing to say so she felt she had 'permission' to leave us. I did not want her to die, but she just could not fight another day.

Mum began groaning as her breathing became harder and spaced further apart. Then she opened her eyes—only slightly—and looked into mine. My beautiful Mum had not looked at me since Friday morning and it was now early Sunday morning. This was the last time we would see each other. I moved up close to her face and stroked her hair. I did not take my eyes off hers and I smiled. She managed to smile back and just stared at me, trying to say something—I'm not sure what. I wish I knew. If she was thinking, I wonder what her thoughts were?

I made every effort to stay in control of the moment. I was not going to cry yet, just in case I became a blubbering out-of-control mess and I didn't want to upset her. I took over the role of main carer long ago and I wasn't going to let her down now. I repeated to her that she could let go. Small tears rolled out of my eyes, but I smiled and comforted her as she kept her gaze firmly on me. Then her eyes began to look different. They went from a lovely, clear hazel colour to a foggy, empty appearance.

The nurses came in to see how Mum was doing and just as they went to give her a little more morphine, her whole body collapsed and she stopped breathing. My heart sank. I gazed up at the nurses with a look of panic and told them she had stopped breathing. They said she would take her final breaths very soon and then it would be over. They then quietly stepped out the room.

Just as the nurses said, Mum took two or three final gasps for air. It was one of the most frightening times of my life. If I could just have 'fixed' her and kept her with me I would have, but this was way out of my control. So I just sat there—keeping that firm grip on her hand— and let her slip away. It was my duty to do so. She released my hand. I said over and over, 'I love you'. And then she was gone. Silence. For the first time in my whole life, I was without my mum.

3 August 2008

I just feel so sorry for my beautiful mum. I can't believe she is gone. I HATE IT. I can't feel her anywhere. I don't know where in this world she is. I want her to be with me. I HOPE SHE IS OK. I want to hug her. I love her. I miss her. When will my heart rest? When will it stop feeling so heavy? Will I ever get over this feeling? I feel sick. SO, SO, SO SICK.

I just sat there—numb—not sure what to do. I looked at my uncle and he said, 'She's gone now. It's all over'. I knew this, but I couldn't believe it. This was the moment that I had been dreading for three years. It had actually happened. It wasn't a bad dream. I howled. Years worth of emotion poured out. I laid my head on Mum's arm and cried and cried. Everything felt immediately different.

After a short time, the nurses knocked on the door and asked if I wanted them to 'clean her up'. Family would be coming to say their final goodbyes. So the nurses thought it would be nice to put Mum in a fresh nightie, brush her hair and give her some dignity. Mum was never one for fuss—so already I could imagine her rolling her eyes—but I said yes.

As the nurses attended to Mum, I went off to phone my brother in Japan. The phone didn't have to ring long. 'Hello', he said very quietly. He knew what I was about to tell him. 'Hi Jim, Mum's gone', I replied, bursting into tears. 'Oh, are you OK?' he asked, sounding defeated. 'Yeah, I'm just sad', was all I could manage. Jim seemed so far away. He was far away. I told him that Mum went comfortably and with a smile.

Mum's final smile was such a lovely lasting memory for me to hold. I guess this was Mum's way of comforting me, her daughter—letting me know that she was going to be all right. So typical of my mum.

After a while—as many phone calls and a stream of family in disbelief arrived—I was told it was OK to go back into Mum's room. I asked everyone if I could go in alone for a while. I walked down the long corridor with my eyes fixed on Mum's door. I felt a kaleidoscope of emotions: nervousness, confusion, exhaustion and devastation. I slowly opened the door, apprehensive about what I was going to see.

Mum was lying in the bed with the blankets pulled up high. A rolled-up face washer was placed under her chin to keep her jaw firmly closed. On her large, tumour-filled tummy rested some framed photos that had sat in her room and a long-stemmed flower from one of the many bunches she'd been given. It did look strange. She would not have approved at all. I guess though, it broke the overall doom and gloom of the scene.

The room was so quiet. All I could hear was the beating of my pounding heart. I pulled a chair up next to the bed and just stared at Mum's face. My eyes scanned her, knowing that this was my last chance to look at my mum. I wanted to imprint her in my memory: her skin tone; her ear shape; her wrinkles; the way her hair always parted in the same place; the shape of her nose, which is also my nose and my sons' nose; her many freckles that covered her pale skin. I told her that I loved her, that I already missed her and that I hoped she was happy with everything I had done for her. With that I stood up, leaned over and gave her already black, cold lips a kiss. What now?

3 August 2008

I'm sitting on the outside step of Mum's house. It's 5am and I'm having a big glass of wine and a cigarette. I know if Mum is looking at me right now she will not be approving, but I'm sure she will let it slide—just this once.

I'm exhausted. I can't stop my body from shaking. I'm not cold, I think it's just devastation. Tim is with me, holding me tight. We are just sitting quietly. I take comfort in writing all of this down. I'm trying to process what has just happened. Never have I felt such emptiness. I feel like I am a shell with nothing inside. My stomach hurts so much. Or is it my heart? I feel sick. I'm lost. I want my mum...

In the wee hours of the morning, I finally took myself off to bed. The bed in the spare room at Mum's house. This room was once my childhood bedroom—the room in which I would sit and sulk as an ungrateful teenager after being told off. As I lay there, the birds were singing their morning song. The sun was starting to rise on the first day without my beautiful mum in this world. While my life had just been devastated, others would be embarking on a normal day. Everything happening outside my window was exactly as it was yesterday—and every other day. For me though, it would never be the same.

I sobbed myself to sleep. This was a primal crying—a crying that alerted Tim to squeeze me tight and just go with the rhythms of my body as it broke down from grief and exhaustion. Eventually I went to sleep—finally at peace, for the moment at least.

When I woke, only seconds passed before I was reminded that my new reality was not a bad dream. My reality now did not involve my mother.

# Chapter 10

The days following Mum's death were full of meetings, funeral details, well-wishes, sympathy, cards, flowers—so many bunches of flowers—and sadness. Far too much sadness. I felt so alone. I was the only one who could deal with the hurt that I was feeling. That was the most frightening reality.

4 August 2008
I'm broken. Literally...

5 August 2008
I'm positive that if my boys didn't rely on me, I would completely lose it. I am barely hanging on. I just don't know what to do with myself, with my sadness. I don't want to do anything. It is just so hard to get out of bed and pretend as though I care about anything, but I have to. I'm so deeply and morbidly sad. I have never felt so afraid to be me in all of my life. I wish that I could just switch the hurt off, if only for a minute. I need a little break. If only I could just hide somewhere—away from my boys—and cry for days and days...

Nobody could fix it for me. Nobody but me could take the steps to heal what literally felt like a damaged heart. It was unbearable. In the days following Mum's passing, I went into flight mode—running on adrenaline. The reality of my loss had thankfully become camouflaged by the list of duties that I had to attend to. I felt as though I was in control of all that had to be done. As long as I was kept busy, I managed.

My boys were my strength. They knew their Nanny had died, but they were so amazing. They allowed me to come and go with minimal fuss, they helped around the house, they smothered me in hugs and kisses and they behaved beautifully. They were taking very good care of me—something I desperately needed after spending so long taking care of Mum. She would have been so proud of them.

My husband kept me sane. He went with the flow of tears, anger, adrenaline and disbelief. I was in a constant shift of emotion that he handled so well. This kind of emptiness was something I had never felt before. I wasn't quite sure what to do, so I set my sights on making sure that Mum's funeral was perfect. That, at least, was something that I *could* control.

8 August 2008

Mum's funeral was yesterday. It went well. Jim and I were able to deliver heartfelt speeches. I got quite teary through mine. Jim spoke beautifully and got upset at the end. He looked so alone—a boy who has lost his mum. A boy who still needs his mum.

It felt so weird that Mum's coffin was right in front of me the whole time. I felt nothing. I knew that 'she' wasn't in there. But where is she? I'm so afraid of the coming week. I'm not very busy and I'm going to have more time to think about the enormity of her never coming back. It's slow and steady for me now—one foot in front of the other. Time to begin figuring out how to live without Mum and heal my heart, all of our hearts if that's possible. I will never forget my beautiful mum and I will miss her terribly...

Days blurred into each other. I dragged myself out of bed in the morning, grateful that I had to get the boys up and off to school and their activities. These routines forced me to face the day. I had no energy though—no interest even in showering or brushing my teeth. I barely ate, as I was constantly nauseous. Instead, I got through the days by drinking far too much coffee and smoking way too many cigarettes.

For a while, I stayed away from people who I knew. I could not deal with any more sympathy. I knew that everyone meant well, but I was not OK and couldn't pretend to be. Tears streamed down my face with no warning. I had come to realise that only very few people could handle the reality of deep, dark grief. So many others ran a mile and I didn't want to make anyone uncomfortable. As such, I remained under the radar for some time.

Food shopping was a nightmare for me. Everywhere I turned I saw mums and daughters shopping together, just as Mum and I had done so many times in the past. Oh how I had taken it all for granted back then. Tears would well up, but I was learning how to bury the pain and dry up the tears—a skill that came in handy so many times over.

14 August 2008
Dad rang today. He is so sad. I don't quite know what to say to him. I just don't have the strength to build him up this time. He said that I sound exactly like Mum. Once I finished the phone call, I bawled my eyes out. I miss Mum so much. I want to talk to her...

26 August 2008
I had a dream last night and Mum was in it. I was sitting at the table in her house and she came and sat with me.

She looked well and was wearing a bright red shirt. I felt quite shocked because, even in my dream, I knew that she had died. All the same, we just started talking. I said, 'Um, but you died'. She said, 'Yeah, I know'. Then I said, 'We had your funeral and it was nice. I'm sure it was just as you wanted'. She agreed then said, 'I tell you what. I woke up this morning, opened my eyes and I thought "Oh fucking hell, I'm still here!"'. Is this Mum's way of reaching out and telling me to stop worrying? Of telling me that she is OK and she is relieved it's all over? I've never experienced a dream like this in my life…

Each day that passed would deliver me a little bit more strength—perhaps from Mum, herself. I began to allow myself some quiet time to process the loss. I would let my mind go as far as acknowledging that she was no longer around in body, but I could go no further than that. The reality of never being with her again was too huge to comprehend.

One of the hardest adjustments I had to make was not being able to call Mum. At times, I would actually grab the phone and start dialling her number—only to be brought back to the harsh reality that she was not going to answer. Each night as I drifted off to sleep, I would wish so hard that Mum would visit me in my dreams so that we could chat. That was all I wanted—just one more chat with my mum. I already had so much to tell her…

3 September 2008

Mum has been dead for four weeks today. A part of me has also been missing since then. I'm trying so hard to go through the motions of life, but I am still so deeply sad. I have developed a very unhealthy habit of drinking wine to mask the real emotion I am feeling. Wine helps me to relax *a bit, but I am relying on it more and more. I'm just not ready to deal with reality yet.*

*10 September 2008*

*God, I miss Mum so much. I feel as though all the emotion is just sitting in my throat, desperate to come out. I've cried a million tears—surely I have no more left? At times, I can't quite grasp the fact that she is not coming back. It's so final. It doesn't seem real. Does everyone who loses someone they love think this way? It's phenomenal that a person can live and exist, buy things, learn things, do things—and then they are gone. Is life just all about having a bloody good time and that's it? I wish I could hug Mum. I want to feel her warmth.*

Over the coming weeks, I was in house selling mode. Mum's house was to be emptied and sold. As I was Power of Attorney, it was up to me. Again, I thrived in the busyness of it all—as this kept me from thinking too much—but it was harrowing to part with Mum's possessions. If I could keep it all, I would have. In reality, though, I knew that she would have been so cross with me if I had hung onto silly things just because they were hers.

I made sure that family and friends took what they wanted to remember Mum by and I did the same. Bit by bit, as I sifted through her treasured belongings and cried rivers of tears, the house became less her home—less the house I grew up in—and more of a shell. Over the time it took to prepare Mum's house for market, I started coming to terms with its inevitable sale. When the sale eventually went through, I knew it was meant to be. My brother and I could not manage to continue maintaining Mum's home, so selling it was our only option.

It was so hard to close the door on the home in which I had spent my childhood; my rebellious teenage years; early motherhood; and shared many cups of tea with Mum. It made things all the more final.

15 October 2008

Today is my birthday. My first one ever without Mum and I'm SO emotional. I feel like staying in bed all day and feeling sorry for myself. I'm angry today. It's not fair that my mum is dead. I miss her every day—more and more as each day passes—but today I feel so sad and heavy. Mum always really made my day special. I wish I could bring her back. I know that I can't. Happy birthday to me—whatever!

18 October 2008

Jack is really angry. Tonight he just lost it. He screamed, cried and then stormed off to his room where he began bashing his fists on the floor in an absolute rage. I yelled out to Tim, as I was really scared about what was happening. I grabbed Jack and clung on really tight. He just cried and cried. So did I. He yelled 'I want Nanny' over and over. All I could say was, 'Me too'.

This would break Mum's heart. She would hate to see the torment that Jack is going through. He is only eight years old. It's not fair that he has to feel such sadness and confusion. I don't know how to deal with this. Is cuddling him enough or should I seek out some counselling for him? On top of all this, he is being bullied at school so his world just feels very sad. I need to fix this for him but I feel so broken myself. What can I do to help him?

# Chapter 11

Often I would wake exhausted. I could only assume that I had dreamed of Mum, as I felt as though I had cried and cried during my sleep. I would then spend hours processing my emotions, trying to lift myself from the pits of grief to feel somewhat happy. I just wanted to be with Mum. I often wondered where she was and what she was doing. I wished I could just spend one more day with her.

22 October 2008

Oh the peaks and troughs. Last night I had one of those 'no warning' meltdowns. I cried and sobbed like I did when my mum had just died. Sadly, my unhappiness last night triggered a wave of built-up tears from my boys too.

Kye went off quietly to his room, so I went to see if he was all right. I found him sitting on his bed. He looked beat. I asked if he was OK and he said, 'I miss Nanny'. I hugged him so hard and told him that I did too. Joshi came in and said, 'It's OK, she will be back soon'. Kye replied by yelling, 'NO! She will never come back!'. Off I went again. It's in these situations that you can literally feel your heart hurt, ache and break.

I managed to calm Kye down, but then I heard Jack sobbing in another room with Tim. I went to him and told him it was OK to cry. I put Jack in our bed and got ready for bed myself. We cuddled each other, had a solid cry and then fell asleep, exhausted. When, if ever, will this get any easier?

Not only was I trying to process my own grief, but it had become very clear that my boys were suffering too. Their little brains could not fathom what had happened. I blamed myself, as I didn't think that I had prepared them for the loss of their 'Nanny'. I'd been very careful to protect them emotionally from the ups and downs of Mum's cancer journey, but perhaps I hadn't given them the opportunity to properly say goodbye to Mum. All I knew was that, at the time, I thought that I was doing my best. There was no way of knowing how it was all going to unfold.

10 November 2008

I have these moments that take me quite by surprise. Even while I am engrossed in a book or a movie, I suddenly think of Mum. My thought and reaction process goes something like this: I think, 'Mum was 56 when she died'; I get hot flushes; my heart races; I start to feel angry, sad and helpless.

I wish Mum could watch the boys grow into men. I wish she could have had only 20 years more. That's not too much to ask is it? A lot of women live to the age of 76. I have so many moments in which I am reminded of her. If I see grandmothers with their grandchildren, I almost lose my shit! I doubt that I will ever come to terms with losing my mum. I know that other people have had far worse tragedies in their lives but, for me, this is the worst that I have had to deal with. I just hope that, as time passes, I come to terms with it.

21 November 2008

I think I may need to find a grief counsellor. I need to say and express so much—to cry, yell, vent and scream 'IT'S NOT FAIR!' 100 times over. I think I will gain a lot from letting it all out and will, hopefully, also get some good advice as to how I can turn things around.

My emotions are always sitting in my throat and this is weighing me down. I'm smoking a lot and drinking quite a bit of alcohol. I don't want to live life like this anymore. I am not being a very good role model for my boys and I know Mum would want me to be happier and healthier than I currently am. I feel as though I am making her sad by being so sad myself. So silly— even when she is no longer here, I want to make her proud. I loved her so much.

I remember that when I was little, I would lie by Mum's feet and kiss the soles of her shoes. Sure this may seem like a strange thing to do, but she was clearly my hero from a very young age.

13 December 2008

I've had a reality check—one that I desperately needed. Last night, I went out with two of my best friends and I had way too much to drink. My friends saw that I was in a bad way so they dragged me out of the club we were at and flagged down a taxi. I remember sitting in the cab feeling so, so sad.

Once we safely arrived at my friend's house, I just broke down. I cried and sobbed. I let go of all the torture swirling in my head and my heart. My friends cried with me and allowed me the safety of their trusting friendship to just release all of my sadness. I'm so grateful to have such amazing women close to me—who are like my sisters—to help me through this tough phase.

Now, the morning after, I feel so sick. I'm sick of feeling so sad. I'm making a promise with myself right now that I will be more kind. I owe it to my family to start cheering up. I have to try and want to feel alive again. I have to shake off the feeling of guilt that I carry about wanting to be happy. It is time to take some responsibility for my emotions and move forward.

As a mother I didn't have the luxury of continually staying up late and drinking too much, then waking up each morning feeling like I'd been hit by a truck. This was how I had been existing, but now I had to take positive steps to begin the healing process. Making these changes was essential for my family and for myself.

I searched high and low for a grief counsellor. I knew that this next step was an important one and would force me to face the many emotions that needed addressing. Yet it was rather frightening to know that I was going to open up about my mother's death and discuss what I had been through. It was not a case of wanting to, however, it was simply that I had to. My own health and the hearts of my family members depended on it.

20 January 2009

I'm exhausted! I've just had the most intense counselling session. I waltzed in there feeling bright, even wondering if I should bother attending. Then, in no time, the emotions just rose up and spilled out.

My counsellor and I discussed how usually, when we

don't like a situation we are in, we change the environment. In such a situation like losing Mum though, I'm unable to change the environment I'm in. The fact that she died will never go away. I will never be able to fix it. I can, however, change my internal response to the environment that I am in.

Currently, I choose to drink and smoke to disguise my pain and anger. I use these substances to make myself numb. If I'm feeling anxious, I reach for a cigarette. In the time it takes me to have a smoke, the feelings have gone again and I'm back to normal. What I am creating by doing this, though, is an unstable wave of heavy emotion. I'm not dealing with the core emotions, which is why they rise up at the most unexpected times. I have to stop and face these random moments in order for the pain to settle and for these moments to stop being so frightening...

Each day would see me battle a different mood. Even within one short day, I would ride a roller coaster of confusing emotions. I'd try so hard to be bright and happy in the mornings for my boys, as I believed it was unhealthy for them to start their day with negativity. Some days, though, it was just plain impossible. Even burning toast would send me into a spin. I was weighed down with hurt. I felt so sorry for my mum. Every time I saw a group of middle-aged ladies having coffee, or grandmothers spending time with their precious grandchildren, the emotions would take me on a ride of utter sadness.

I read in a book someone gave me about grief that '*depression is an unwelcome guest who will arrive unannounced and stay for as long as it wants, so you might as well pull up a chair and sit comfortably by the fire together as there is no point running away*'. This rang so true to me. I don't know if depression was the issue, but I was certainly sad and it was very hard to lighten my mood.

2 February 2009

I'm on a huge 'downer' at the moment. I have felt so emotional all day and then I realised that it is six months tomorrow since Mum died. God, I miss her! It still hurts so much.

My poor, darling mum—it doesn't seem right that she won't see her grandsons grow. The boys have changed so much in the past six months. They are already different from how they were the last time she saw them. Teeth have fallen out and new ones are pushing through. They have new achievements that they want to share with her. She has already missed out on so much. It's just not fair.

I picked up Mum's ashes today. I was so nervous about it, but once I had the urn I was OK. I had a peek. The contents were so strange—ashy yet full of clumps. I just sat, staring at the ashes and trying to comprehend that this was my mum. How can life come to this point? It makes no sense...

Sometimes I just catch myself daydreaming, thinking about Mum. I sink into a feeling of doubt over losing her—a disbelief that I won't ever see her again. I miss her too much.

4 March 2009

Last night I saw Coldplay in concert. So many of the songs they played were ones that I'd listened to during the time of Mum's illness. As such, Coldplay's album 'Viva la Vida' has become somewhat of a soundtrack to that part of my life. It's the music I cried to as I drove home after

Mum died. So to see these songs played live was incredibly overwhelming and emotional. There were moments that I could have let go and howled, but I knew it would have got ugly—so I held on. I couldn't do that to the people next to me. It would have been horrifying for them! I have such an ugly cry.

AND THE WORLD
FELT FULL OF
LOVE THAT
DAY

# Chapter 12

As time passed, I was feeling a sense of calm. Bit by bit, slowly and without too many tears, I was beginning to feel peace in my heart. I was allowing myself time to think. I was taking time out to walk and clear my mind. I was granting myself uninterrupted moments where I gratefully reflected on what had happened along the way.

15 March 2009

I'm feeling good. I feel as though I have turned a corner. My heart is not as sore. My counsellor says that psychologists believe we have receptors in our brain that are nourished when we see those that we love and care for. The receptors fire out a want to hear someone's voice or physically see them and when we 'answer' that need, we are fulfilled. When someone we love dies, these receptors still fire out the need but they go unanswered. This causes heartache and confusion but, over time, the receptors learn that they are not going to hear the voice or see the person. Slowly, the need dies off and the intense pain eases.

I think of Mum every day. But now I am finding that when I think of her, I smile. I draw on the nice memories. I focus on the strong, independent, healthy woman that she was. I do truly believe that she is with me all the time.

23 March 2009

Today I was cleaning out a cupboard and came across a book that my mum's past colleagues made her as a retirement gift. It was full of photos of her from her time with them. These are photos that I am not familiar with, so the tears came pouring out! Just when you think they have dried up, they start again. Oh I miss her.

My friend told me recently that she believes that if you need to have a cry about something, then go forth and have a damn good cry! She said that your brain then says, 'OK, we have served that emotion/memory/feeling now. No need to dwell anymore, let's move onto the next one'. I like this interpretation. Tears do run out over certain things. That's the wonderful thing about healing. Eventually I hope to only remember Mum fondly, with less tears.


10 May 2009

My first ever Mother's Day without a mother. It sickens me to be honest and I just can't wait for the day to be over. Frankly, I don't care that I'm a mum today. I just want MY mum.

All I have heard about for weeks is Mothers' Day. On the TV, in magazines—it's all over the shops. Everywhere I look, I see gifts and cards for mothers. I am being told over and over again to 'Make sure that you tell your mum that you love her'. I am no longer in that blessed club. I don't have a mum to buy gifts for. I don't have a mum to spoil. I just can't bare it. Bring on tomorrow!

19 May 2009

I am noticing that I'm feeling a little bit happier with each day. Sadness comes, but it comes less often and is no longer so consuming. It's been just over nine months since Mum died. I can't believe it's been that long. When Mum was alive, we spoke every day. Nine months is a bloody long time to not have spoken to her. That's the hardest part. It would be lovely to just have a chat. When I long to hear her voice, I replay her answering machine message in my head. I don't know why, but it has stuck with me and is as clear in my memory as the last time I heard it.

I was waking with hope and happiness. I was giving myself permission to move forward. Mum would have wanted this, just as I would have wanted to see my children move on from being so sad. I was aware of all the beauty around me, even if Mum was not a part of it. I felt as though it was up to me to live life for the both of us and not waste it feeling so glum all the time. The goal was to try to focus on positive things only and shut down the negative thoughts. It was all controlled by my mind and attitude. Now was the time for me to begin a new way of living. Ultimately, it was my choice. No time was to be wasted feeling sorry for myself.

27 May 2009

It's Mum's 57th birthday tomorrow. I'm not sure what I am supposed to do. I think about her all the time, so there's no need to take time out to remember her. I often catch myself wondering what journey Mum is on. I wonder where she is—if anywhere—and if she is OK. I miss her so much. Especially in the quiet times. I have decided that each year on her birthday, I will splash out on a gorgeous bunch of flowers to celebrate her. Mum loved fresh flowers, as do I, so this tradition will be perfect.

28 May 2009

Happy 57th birthday Mum xxxx

I'm often told that I will receive gifts from Mum as time passes. I've never been sure of what that meant until today. I was at the gym and I ran into a woman that I have known for a while. We got talking and I found out that she also lost her mum to cancer. She was 20 when her mum died and she regrets that her mother was not able to meet her husband or children. Instantly, I realised how blessed I was. My mum left this world knowing who I married and meeting my three boys and loving them. She was happy for me and we shared so many important moments. I need to focus on what I had with Mum, not on what I didn't. So many others are not as lucky. I take the gift of appreciation today. Did Mum place me there, on her birthday, to teach me about gratitude? Maybe...

10 June 2009

Ups and downs! I can never predict it and I'm tired of it. It's 3:03am and I have just been in to Kye and Joshi to settle them both back to sleep. They were both sobbing and saying that they miss their Nanny. I hugged them tight and said 'I do too'. I hate these moments. They are torture. I'm heavy hearted now and feel like I am going to sob. Perhaps I should. I think in these times, Mum must hate seeing us so sad. It must hurt her so much.

Lately I have felt a new wave of emotion. Anger. I'm so angry that my mum had cancer. But I believe that what you put out into the world, you get back. I have felt like the universe has been unfriendly to me lately—clearly due to my own attitude. I can change this. I have done it before. It's time to calm things down a bit, breathe and take care of myself. I need to feel inner peace. I deserve to prioritise myself and make sure that I am receiving what I need to be feeling my best.

Finally, I was beginning to respect who I was. I was proud of everything I had done and how I had coped. I'd managed to support my mother, who was my best friend, to her time of death. Then I'd stepped immediately back into the role of being a mother myself, to three young boys who desperately needed me. I nurtured them, all while battling extreme sadness. Instead of giving in to grief, I rose to each and every challenge to come out strong and so in love with my life. For the first time in my 33 years, I felt in charge of myself and bloody happy to be in my own skin. I still had quite a journey ahead but so far, so good.

26 June 2009

I have purposely been spoiling myself lately! Long baths, chocolate, good books. I feel better for it too, although my butt has spread quite a bit. I'm thinking about Jack's birthday and how I can make it really special for him. Hopefully I can provide him with lots of fun, even while knowing all too well that the next day is the anniversary of Mum's death. I'm apprehensive about it all but, for Jack's sake—especially as he misses her so much—his birthday has to be amazing. I'm not sure how I am going to feel around that time. I can't believe it's nearly been a whole year...

Life was beginning to feel normal—nice and fun. I soaked up the happy, carefree environment that we had missed so desperately for so long. There was no denying that we all still missed Mum terribly, but we were welcoming happiness back into our world—and boy, was it a nice change!

3 July 2009

I love that my boys are happy. There has been so much sadness for them—it's so good to see them joyful. As I write this, they are blissfully humming away as they go about their business. Mum used to say that humming was a true sign of happiness. She loved their little songs.

I was driving with Joshi yesterday and he said, 'Mum, Kye makes me smile'. I said, 'Do you smile when you think of Kye?'. He grinned a big wide smile and replied, 'yeah'. I'm so blessed. I have so much goodness in my life—so much that fills my heart with warmth. I think the important thing is to stop and take notice of the magic that surrounds us all. Sometimes we can be so busy that the magic is missed, but the everyday moments are so worth treasuring. I never had this awareness before Mum got sick. I was blind to life's beauty. She taught me so many important life skills. I wonder if it was her plan?

20 July 2009

The one year anniversary of Mum's death is looming—in two weeks to be exact. Sometimes, the reality of it all is too much to bear and I choose not to think much about it. This is the only way I know to prevent myself from dwelling. I see grandmothers with their grandkids all the time and it still hurts so much—it probably always will. I think I'm extra raw emotionally at the moment because of the time of year.

I feel strongly, though, that Mum is working her 'magic' within me. It sounds strange, but I do believe that she is a part of me and plays a role in the choices I make. I feel calmer and more confident. I feel more sure of who I am and what I stand for. I feel her strength, especially in the times where the boys need my compassion. I have a sense of gratitude that I never had before. I hear the quiet sound of the wind whooshing through trees. I appreciate warm, sunny days and long walks. I savour a strong cup of tea. I take time to stop and experience what is around me with open eyes. I never cared for these moments in the past—I was too busy and unaware. I was selfish and only thinking of myself. Nothing was ever good enough. This past year has seen the most significant change in me. Some haven't liked it, but most have supported me as I've reclaimed my soul after it was trampled by grief. I have accepted Mum's 'gifts' along the way. I'm just so thankful for the lessons she taught me and continues to teach me. I was so lucky to have had her as my mum.

2 August 2009

Mission accomplished! Today is Jack's 9th birthday and as last year's birthday was absolutely horrendous for him, this one has been epic. He is on top of the world, feeling happy and very spoilt—just as he should be. He has been such a pleasure to celebrate with. He's so grateful and willing to share all of his new presents with his brothers. It's been mad and lots of fun, but I am satisfied that we pulled this off with nothing but smiles.

Tomorrow does not need to be sad. I've thought a lot about 'this time last year' and I won't lie, it was the worst time of my life thus far. But, in a way, I have made it all better by spoiling my child on his birthday—something that was impossible to do last year. I'm sure that, over time, this will all get easier. I understand that it is OK to celebrate without Mum here. I'm sure she is sharing our moments somehow, smiling her wide, beautiful smile.

# Chapter 13

3 August 2009
One year.

I decided to honour Mum by planting her favourite tree—that we had successfully relocated from her yard into ours—and scattering some of her ashes under it. So off I went. I found the perfect spot and began to dig, dig, DIG! All the while, a police helicopter kept circling above. I did wonder if they were concerned about what I was doing. I was, in fact, burying my mother in my backyard—but legally! It brought a smile to my face, as I knew Mum would have loved the irony. I felt like I was in one of those funny English comedies that we always loved to watch together. All I needed was Dawn French or Patsy and Eddie to come bursting in. The wind was a bit blowy and some of Mum did 'take off'—again I smiled, as we had discussed wind factor and how it would be funny if she flew back into my face—but thankfully, the majority of 'her' went where I wanted it to. I sat there for a while and just chatted to my mum. Then, when it felt right, I began covering the ash with soil and watered the tree into the ground. It was comforting that a part of her remained with me in my yard. It felt right.

20 August 2009
My thoughts just trail off sometimes. I start with the reality of Mum's death. She is, in fact, NOT on a holiday

as it sometimes seems. She is dead. Gone. Sadness kicks in. Heartache stabs once more. Then I begin to ponder what on earth life is all about. I think it must be about making your journey one of the best possible quality: to influence others with your good deeds; to have zest for life; to have ambitions; to encourage others around you to make the most out of their own lives. That's what makes all the worry, the hard work and the sacrifices worth it.

I think when opportunity strikes, you must snatch it and run like the wind. Be the best person you can be and live your best life. I think we must love and be proud of who we are—always standing up for our beliefs. I know that it's not important to be liked by everyone—in fact, it's impossible. To love yourself is the most important thing—another 'gift', perhaps? I don't know, but I'm just taking it all as it comes!

10 September 2009

My brother is in town, so yesterday we set the remainder of Mum's ashes free. Mum had requested to have them spread in the bay and I'm so pleased to have done as she wished. We set out on the boat and thankfully, it was the most gorgeous spring day. The sun shone so bright for us. Tim parked the boat way out in the bay and Jim and I opened the container and let Mum go. We both agreed that Mum's ashes are just that and she, herself, is in and all around us.

Once the container was emptied, the ashes all came together under the water and literally 'swam off'. It was astonishing to witness. We continued to watch as the light colour of Mum's remains swam further and further, away all the while staying firmly together. They dipped and swirled with the swell of the water until we could no longer see them. I was squinting so hard to keep them in sight but, eventually, I had to let her go. She was well and truly free.

We clanged our beers and yelled to Mum that we love her to the moon and back. I'm so thankful to have been able to share that moment with Jim. It's something we will never forget. It was a beautiful, calming way to farewell our mum.

12 September 2009

I'm sitting here tonight, reflecting on the past few days and I feel so inspired. I feel that, in the time since Mum died, I have experienced so much as a woman, as a daughter, as a mother and as a friend. Many of these experiences have been life-changing challenges. Each and every day I grow stronger. I miss Mum terribly and I always will, but I appreciate all that she has given me.

I am grateful for the journey that followed Mum's death. The journey that took me from the absolute pits of grief and loss following an event that destroyed me internally and forced me to re-build—almost like a re-birth of sorts. I could not give up. I had three young boys who were equally devastated and they needed me to keep them secure. It's been the toughest challenge of my life but, when I stand in front of the mirror, I love what I see. I am me. I am a combination of all that I loved about my mum, as well as every little lesson I have learned in the past year.

I have resilience now. Whereas once I was a weak-minded quitter, I am now a person who does not believe in the word 'can't'.

I have compassion. I used to care very little for others and mostly for myself, but now I feel so deeply for those that I love.

I have respect. Everyone is worthy of his or her best life. Everybody deserves a chance to shine.

I have ambition. I used to just mope along, waiting to be handed the world on a plate without much direction. But now—just try and stop me! There is so much I want to achieve, perhaps too much.

I have self-love. I am comfortable in my own skin. I have so much to offer and I love who I am and what I stand for. I believe in myself and feel very proud of all that I have achieved.

I have gratitude. Once upon a time, I never took any notice of anything outside myself. It was all about me. I now have the gift of seeing and hearing life's little treasures: the brightness of a flower; the sound of a bird's song; a beautiful sky. There is so much beauty. It surrounds us all—you just have to see it.

I am a confident mother. Once, I could not make a decision without the guidance of my own mum. Now I believe that the choices I make with my heart are the best and so far, I've done ok.

I am an attentive and supportive wife. I'm relieved

that Tim saw something in me worth fighting for and remained by my side during the tough times. No longer do I make our relationship all about me. It is about us, our delicious boys and the connectedness we share together. I'm very blessed.

I look in the mirror and question who I would be if Mum were still alive and healthy. I would not have had the soul-shifting upheaval I've undergone. I would not have had the desperation to improve my life. I would not have been so lucky as to have taken on board some of life's most special lessons. Life is precious. It has no guarantees and can be taken from anyone in the blink of an eye. Life is for living.

Things that I used to worry about, I no longer give any of my time to. I make grand plans and move heaven and earth to achieve my goals. I don't believe that there is a limit to what I can achieve and I will not let anything get in my way. I don't think this is selfishness. I think wallowing in my own misery in my 'past' life was selfish. Now, though, I hope to sprinkle some of my joy and excitement on those with who I surround myself—especially my boys.

The journey I underwent in losing my mum is something I do not wish on anyone. If I could, I would rewind time and keep her safe from cancer with some magical miracle cure. I'm sure all people who have lost someone they adore would do the same. But this is the real world and shitty things happen. All I can do is not let her death be an event that happened in vain. I will live my most wonderful life, in honour of Mum and of others I have loved who also had their precious lives cut short. In times of sorrow, I will remind myself of their sacrifices and shake up my soul. I'm happy, healthy and alive. That's to be celebrated. Carpe Diem...every single Diem!

# Chapter 14
## A letter to my mum

10 March 2014

To my darling mum,

It's been almost six years since we last met. That's a long time. I miss you so much—more than I ever have. But the pain in my heart has eased. I smile, I laugh, I dream and I allow myself to achieve without you by my side.

I thank you for the strength that you have filled me with, for the courage that I have developed and for the gratitude that pours from my soul each and every day. It is because of you that I am the person I am today. I wish that we could meet again. I think you would be so proud. I can't help but think that I am the woman now that you so longed for me to be. I wish you could witness that.

I took the plunge and had that longed-for fourth child that I always discussed with you. Yep, another boy—you would have giggled—and he is divine. Lovely little Oliver came to us on 11 December 2011.

During Ollie's birth, I knew that you were with me. At the point where I felt as though I could take no more, I called on you to help me and I believe that you got me through. I felt an extra surge of strength that pulled me through one of the toughest labours that I have endured. I have no explanation other than the reassurance that you guided me when I needed it most.

Little Ollie has the most delicious cheeks that I know you would have nuzzled into. He would have smiled at having you so close and being held safely in your warm, loving arms. There is a photo of you in our dining room and he points to it and says 'Nanny'. It melts my heart every time. He is certainly spoilt rotten by us all!

You would be so in awe of the older boys. They have changed so much since you all last met—too much. Adult teeth have grown and changed their whole appearance. Hair styles are a priority. They are so tall and athletic, obsessed with their sports and hobbies. They still insist on sitting together on the sofa, refusing to move despite being desperate for their own personal space. It's a sign of love and togetherness I suppose. I celebrate it rather than get mad when they start snapping at each other! They sure can get cranky, but they really do love and respect each other and get along well.

You said that I would make a great nurse and caring for you certainly got me thinking. So I followed my dream and now I officially have a career in nursing—and I love it! I gain so much from caring for others. I know in my heart that this is what I am meant to do and I'm happy. I make a difference to so many and that is exactly how I want to devote my time in this life.

Often in my job, I meet old ladies who remind me of you—well, what I imagine you to be if you were granted the fortune to grow old. It stops me in my tracks and can sometimes hurt my heart. But I just go on, knowing that you left this life with a sense of calm and acceptance. This is what lifts me up and guides me through those tough times.

I wish I could hear your voice, Mum—just once more. To sit at a café with you and just chat about current events and the goings-on with my boys. Oh, I just wish to do this one more time.

I don't know where I am headed from here, but that is the magic and beauty of life. What I do know is that I can do anything I set my heart to. There is so much that I hope to accomplish and I am genuinely excited by life. I share my life with the most amazing man who I know you adored and we truly are best friends—kindred spirits.

My perfect life would be having you here to share it all with me, but I accept that you aren't and I live in your honour. I think about you every day and I feel your presence in all that I do. I take in all that is around me, just as you taught me to. I live a better version of my life because of you and for that, you are my true hero.

I'm positive that wherever you are and whoever you are with, you are making a difference. I am so proud of you and I feel beyond blessed that in this big, wide world, I was lucky enough to call you my mother. I miss you.

All my love, forever
Your eternally grateful daughter
Leigh xxx

# A letter to you, dear reader

To my sisterhood of motherless mothers,

Firstly, I want to thank you so much for reading about my journey. It means so much to me that you have taken the time to understand my heartache at losing my mother to cancer and at having to go on living without such an integral role model in my life.

I have come to realise over the years since losing my mum that I am not alone. So many are suffering without their own mothers in their life. They too are just trying their best to live on without a mothering influence.

I especially feel a sense of connectedness with other motherless mothers. To remain selfless as a mum must be and to continue to raise needy children, all while desperately yearning for your own mum, are life skills that must not go unnoticed. It is not an easy situation and given the choice, I know without a doubt that we all would give anything to have our mums back.

My main purpose in writing this book is to inspire other women who are battling without their mums to feel strength and hope. I aim to help these brave souls to trust in themselves that they will rise out of the painful grief process.

To my kindred motherless mother—you too, my darling woman, will find a way to go on without the support and wisdom of your own beautiful mother. My wish is that, once the last page of this book has been turned, you will feel uplifted and not alone. I want you to believe in yourself. Know that you are amazing and that your mother is watching you with an abundance of love and pride. You must acknowledge that grief has no limit. There is not a switch to turn it off and your journey to feeling whole again will take as long as is needed.

Above all, I want you, my fellow motherless warrior woman, to be kind to yourself. You will never have it all figured out. No-one ever does. But you will have an ability to rise up and face what comes your way, as you have fought the toughest of losses and emerged as the most amazing version of you—ready to conquer the world!

Take all that your mother taught you and combine it with what you stand for, then stand tall. Be proud and carve out a delicious life that you genuinely love. Do it for you. Do it for your family. Most of all, do it for your mum.

Remember that whatever form your journey takes, you are not alone. In the following section, kindred motherless mothers each share their story of travelling the path to heartbreaking loss, through coping with the passing of their beloved mum then forging forward to step back into the sunshine of their lives, without their mum by their side. I hope these stories comfort you with a sense of sisterhood while inspiring and uplifting you on your own journey.

Much love and strength,
Leigh xxx
P.S. Remember, you are not alone.

Without our mothers

A collection of stories from
motherless mothers

# Jo's story

## 45 years old, From United Arab Emirates

**On loss:**

'My mum died on Mother's Day, 21 March 1993. I was seven months pregnant with my second son. When Mum died, I was 24 years old and she was 51. As a motherless mother, I missed insights into my own childhood. I was unable to have the answers to simple questions like, "How old was I when I walked?" and "What childhood illnesses did I suffer from?". I have no history, no answers and no-one to ask.'

**On love:**

'I am thankful that my mum was at my wedding, even though she was ill and wearing her wig—though you'd never have known it wasn't her real hair. Mum thoroughly enjoyed herself.

'I am thankful that my mum met one of my children and got to experience being a grandmother, if only for a short time.'

**On remembering:**

'Mum is remembered every Christmas when my children use their Christmas stockings. My mum had my eldest's stocking handmade, so I got the same lady to make my second son's stocking after Mum died. I then made my daughter's stocking to match her brothers' for her first Christmas. Mum's memory lives on each year.'

**On wishing:**
'If I had one more day with my mum, I would ask her all the questions about my childhood. I would introduce her to my children and tell her about their lives. I would just spend quality time with her.'

# Sarah's story

## 37 years old, From UK

**On loss:**

'My mother was diagnosed with breast cancer when I was in my late 20s. In October 2010, she started experiencing pain in her back and hips. Tests in December 2010 revealed that cancer had metastasised into her spine and pelvis. There was nothing that could be done.

'On New Years Eve that same year, my father passed away at home. I found out that I was pregnant with our second child three days after Dad's funeral.

'My husband, myself and our two-year old daughter had lived in a converted barn on my parents' farm so that we could help them out. After about a month of this living arrangement, we decided to move in with Mum.

'Ten days after we moved into my parents' home, Mum was in so much pain that I panicked and rang the doctor. He called an ambulance and she was taken to hospital. I was almost six months pregnant at the time. I spent two days with her while the hospital carried out tests. One of my strongest memories of this whole time is of Mum spending a few hours drifting in and out of sleep with her hand on my belly, feeling her grandchild kicking.

'The hospital tests confirmed that the cancer had spread to Mum's organs and she had very little time left. My sister and I would both visit her twice a day, but she was asleep most of the time and I would usually just sit next to her and cry.

'Mum had been in hospital for about 10 days when it was my husband's 40th birthday. I visited Mum in the morning and she slept through my visit. My husband and I decided to go out for dinner, even though no-one felt much like celebrating. When we got home, I was so tired that I decided not to go back to the hospital and went to bed instead. At 11.45pm that night, I was awoken by the phone. It was a nurse from Mum's hospital ward saying that I needed to come in as soon as possible.

'When my sister and I arrived at the hospital, Mum was neatly tucked up in bed with a red rose on her chest. She had passed away. The hospital doesn't tell you over the phone that someone has died unless you ask. I didn't ask. We sat in the room with Mum for a while, both feeling totally numb but relieved that her pain was finally over.'

**On love:**
'I used to speak to my mum on the phone almost every day. That is what I miss the most. We would talk for hours.'

# Sylvia's story

## 60 years old, From Australia

**On loss:**

'My life as a child was totally centered around my mum. I look back and see how unprepared I was for dealing with something as big as her illness and subsequent death. My mum was the grown-up. Everything that went on in my life, my mum knew about—everything. We saw each other every day. I'm sure she hadn't planned for me to be so reliant on her, but it's just the way it was.

'I had to grow up quickly once my mum was diagnosed with cancer. She carried herself to death with dignity and faith, beyond what I can even explain. Like it is for so many, hers was a journey that was filled with pain and heartbreak but never a sense of hopelessness.

'When my son was born, Mum was quite well and we were hopeful but she still got very tired, though and spent some time in bed each day. One day, with my son lying on her bed, she looked across at this little newborn baby and said to me, "I wonder if I'll get to see him grow up". This shattered me. It was a physical pain that cut to my core.

'It was about a month later that my dad told me the cancer was now in Mum's bones. The prognosis was not good. My heart broke for him, having to tell me that. On 28 October 1977, my gorgeous mum passed away. I wasn't there. I wanted to be there and felt cheated that no one had rung me. I didn't get to say goodbye, to tell her that I loved her or thank her. For years, I felt no closure because of this.'

**On coping:**
'I look back and wonder how I got through it, but I did. I just did. I was a young wife and mum. I had a dad who was grieving and needed me. I had two little children who needed me too plus a baby who never slept, no driver's licence and only a small group of friends. I don't think being a motherless mum made me a better or worse mother, just a different one perhaps.

'Losing my mother was a journey that I was not prepared for and one I didn't know how to navigate. I think it's a journey that everyone has to take on their own and for some, it is harder than others. Something I know for sure is that there does come a time when you can remember your mum with a smile on your face and joy in your heart—and that is a beautiful thing. Our mums deserve that.'

**On wishing:**
'If I could spend one day with Mum now, I would tell her that I loved her so much, that she was a great mum and that I'm sorry I didn't say this more often. I long to hear her broad Irish accent again. I would give her a huge hug and kiss (because I wasn't good at that back then either) then tell her about her grandchildren and great grandchildren, because that is what she would want to hear about! She would also love to hear about my craft business. I often feel she is looking over me.'

# Melinda's story

## 29 years old, From Australia

**On loss:**
'In October 1995, Mum complained of a sore back. Tests were run and it was revealed that cancer had returned to her spine, lungs, liver and brain. Although Mum's illness took over our lives, I will never forget her bravery, strength and courage throughout the ensuing six months. She still took great care of us and made sure to create for us many wonderful memories of our time with her. My mum died on August 12 1996, aged 36. I was 11 years old.

*"You know that it's ok to cry and don't let anyone tell you otherwise. Let it all out. It will take time, but it will get easier. I love you. I will always be here for you. Just look for me in your dreams and talk to me in your prayers. I will always be right by your side.",* said my mother in a letter that she wrote before she died.'

**On coping:**
'Here I am. A mum. A motherless mum of two babies. Being a mum is the hardest thing I have ever had to do and doing it without my mum makes it even harder! Obviously it is also the most beautiful time of my life, but not being able to share it with my mother weighs heavily on my heart.

'Sometimes I think that I am not coping, that I am falling apart. I think, "I can't do this", but I then get through it. I remember that each day is a new day and I am doing the best I can, just as my mum asked me to do.

'My mum's influence did not die with her. Her warmth, courage, strength, values, morals and determination live on in me. Some days I forget that I am strong. I let my guard down and cry, but crying isn't a sign of weakness. It's an overwhelming sign of strength and a sign from my mum that she is with me, helping me to move forward.'

# Katie's story

## 31 years old, From UK

**On loss:**
'When I was 12 years old, I lost my mum to breast cancer. Being a motherless mother has been one of the most challenging parts of motherhood for me so far.'

**On coping:**
'I became a mum at 27 years old to a beautiful baby girl. I'll never forget the moment at my 12 weeks dating scan when I was told that my baby's due date was 17 November, the date that would have been my mum's 53rd birthday. I always knew that Mum would be a part of my journey into motherhood whether she was here or not. But that moment really brought it home to me that, wherever Mum was, she was with me. It was a really special moment.

'In raising my own daughters, I often think back to how my mum was when she was raising my sister, brother and I. Little things like "no" meaning no and sticking to what you say. It gives me so much comfort to think that she'd be saying to me, "You're doing ok".

'I also carry Mum's values with me. I may have only had her in my life for 12 years, but I learnt so much from her in that short time: how to be a good person; how important it is to be trustworthy and loyal; how to always try to see the positive in a situation; and to be true to yourself. Mum was such an inspiration to me and I am so truly grateful that I had her at all, even if it wasn't for long.'

**On wishing:**

'If I were to have just one more day with Mum, I honestly don't know what I'd want to do and I don't think I'd care what we did. I'd just spend the day trying to soak up every little moment: her smell; the sound of her voice; her laugh; and her smile. I'd ask for advice. I'd tell her that I love her and that I'm never going to forget her or let the girls forget her—because those are the things that matter to me.'

# Kate's story
## 32 years old, From Australia

**On loss:**
'I lost my mum to malignant melanoma in July 2011, three weeks after my wedding. What should have been the best year of my life suddenly became the worst. In January 2011, Mum felt a lump in her armpit. The doctor thought it was a cyst, but did a biopsy because of her history. It was cancer and it had spread, everywhere.

'I remember going to the oncologist with Mum and Dad. Mum told him that she needed to attend my wedding in September. Mum was so sick that she couldn't come to my dress fitting because of her chemo. She was so, so sick at my hen's night but she was still there. I don't know how she was standing, but she was there.

'We moved our wedding from September to June so that Mum could be there. I never thought she would pass so soon afterwards. Never in my worst nightmares would I have ever thought I would lose my mum before I was 30 and I certainly never thought I would have to navigate motherhood without my beautiful mum there to help. She was only 54 when she passed.'

**On coping:**
'I never thought I'd lose my mum. I never thought I'd ever be a mum. But I never, ever thought I'd be a mum without having my mum around. Despite this though, on my husband's birthday and a day after my mum's birthday, I gave birth to a healthy baby boy. Often at

midnight, when my darling little boy is screaming or when I'm beyond exhausted and don't think I can go on, I think of my mum. I talk to her out loud because I know that, somehow, she sent my little man to me. In fact, she's probably up there laughing about it right now. She sent me a little human that didn't sleep for the first six weeks to teach me that I have strength. She sent me an incredibly 'refluxy', unsettled baby to teach me patience and to think of someone other than myself, to not be so selfish. Then, just when I think I've got this motherhood caper sorted, she sends me a curve ball—just to keep me on my toes.'

# Greer's story

## 38 years old, From Australia

**On loss:**

'My first Mother's Day as a new mum was also my first without my own mum. I was about four months pregnant when we found out she was sick. It was a little over a year from her diagnosis to her death in March 2008.

'I'll always be grateful for those months. Mum got to share in the excitement of my pregnancy and was there in the room when my daughter was born. Despite telling me to bunker down with my new family and say no to visitors, she was one of the first to arrive on my doorstep when I got home from the hospital, grinning cheekily and saying she couldn't stay away. She knew she didn't have long, I guess and she wanted to grab as much time as she could with her newest grandchild.'

**On missing:**

'My little girl started kindergarten this year. Grandparents' day floored me. I was running around like a madwoman, dropping off cakes for the morning tea and dashing back to kindergarten from work for the special lunch. All to try and make it up to my baby that she didn't have a grandparent there to show around and show off. I think she might have been the only one in her class who didn't have a grandparent to attend with her.'

**On coping:**

'I got on with things after Mum died. I went back to work and was busy juggling that with mothering. I think it's in my nature to stay busy and fill the spaces with activity.

'I hit a real slump about three months later, which I put down to reality hitting me hard. The flowers and cards had stopped coming and people had stopped asking how I was. Just at the point everyone expects you to be moving on is when you feel the worst.

'But for all this sadness, I rarely get morose or miserable. Perhaps it's because I've experienced death a lot in my life. Perhaps that does harden you a bit, plus it's my natural inclination to see the sunny side of things.

'When I was a child, the thought of losing my mum would send me into buckets of tears. I'd cry if she went away for a night, so to imagine her being gone for good was all too much to bear. When she was diagnosed the first time, I found myself making deals with an imaginary superpower. "You can have her kidney, but you'll need to let her stay", I'd try to bargain.

'When it actually happened, when we did lose her, life just kept rolling on. I suppose I could have collapsed in a heap and let it all overcome me, but I had a baby who needed me and who needed life to be normal. I remember leaving the hospital late one night, a few days before Mum died. My daughter was tired and unsettled in the back seat. I remember wanting to bawl my eyes out, but I had to focus on the road and I had to sing my baby to sleep. 'Silent Night' was what sent her off. I still sing it to her.'

**On wishing:**

'If I could spend one day with my mum, I'd sit her down with a cuppa (or more likely, a gin and tonic) and drill her for information about what it was like raising us, especially when we were little. Did we continually amaze her? Did she want to tear her hair out? Was she afraid to leave us with carers? Did she worry over every little thing? Did we wake up in the night? Were we early risers or fussy eaters? Did we test her every limit, every day? Was she in awe of us: our beauty, the stuff we did, how funny we were? And you can be guaranteed that while I asked the questions and she delivered her answers, the two of us would be knitting away like a pair of old ducks—just like we did many a night in her last year.'

# Melissa's story

## 38 years old, From Australia

**On loss:**

'In my family, no-one understands that ache I get in my heart when I just need a hug from someone who has loved me from before I was born. No-one understands when I just need someone to come and take over things for me for a bit because it's gotten too hard, or when I just want to hang with someone who knows me inside and out.'

**On coping:**

'People underestimate the importance of mother love and support as an adult and without it, I have found that I am stronger than I ever thought I was. I watch and observe other mother/daughter relationships and take note of the things I admire about them, then I learn from those things. Those moments of self-doubt and loneliness that creep up on me as a mother are banished after I repeat the mantra, "At least I have love".

'Being without a mum is the hardest thing that I have ever done. I truly believe that you always carry that emptiness, that feeling that something is missing—but you adjust. You find other older women who you look to for advice and support. In my case, I use my friend's mum and my mother-in-law as mother role models.

'I read a lot and I listen to others talk about their mothers, then I take the good out of what they say and apply it to my situation. Being a motherless mother has made me a more optimistic, loving and forgiving person. Although I am not happy about my status, I am grateful for the better mother and stronger woman it has made me.'

# Pippa's story

## 41 years old, From Australia

**On loss:**
'When I was seven years old, my life turned upside down. Mum was diagnosed with a brain tumor. I remember her walking with a tripod we called 'Joey'. From there, she progressed to a wheelchair and had more people come to the house to help her. I was in my room one day and suddenly ran downstairs to find out that Mum had just died. No-one had called out—I just knew. The following day, I turned 13.

**On coping:**
'At age 21, I was married and due to have my own baby. I had no idea about babies and no-one to help me in those early days. As a new mum, I made so many mistakes with my son and it wasn't until my first two children were toddlers that I seemed to relax as a parent.

'Being a mum is such a tough job. I've read many books, watched how other mums have done it before me and gone to mothers who have walked through difficult times and learned new strategies from them.'

**On wishing:**
'I have ideas of what a mum would be like. I watch other women with their mums and I feel a pang of loss and jealousy, a yearning for what I have lost.'

# Sarah's story

## 40 years old, From UK

**On loss:**

'As a child, I adored my mum. We were very close. When she was diagnosed with cancer in 2001, I was absolutely devastated. The prospect of life without Mum was unthinkable.

'Over the years, as she became more ill, my husband and I adapted our lives around her. I would often take her to chemo appointments or to see the oncologist. I saw her deterioration intensify and yet I was desperate for her to live.

'In May 2010, Mum died. I miss her terribly. Throughout her illness I had called her every day. I had helped her with her shopping, her house and her life. Now she was gone. She was my mother and my friend and I have never stopped missing her.'

**On missing:**

'As my children have grown, I have wanted to call Mum so many times to ask her for advice or hear her reassurances. I find myself wavering in my parenting when the school tells me one of the girls might be struggling in something or that they have achieved an award. Where is Mum to help me?'

**On coping:**

'It occurred to me that, as a mother, we don't die really. We pass on our love, our experiences and our knowledge to our children so that they can pass it on to their children. So from the devastation of losing Mum, I try to remember that it is my job to pass on her gentleness, her love, her guidance and her strength.

'Instead of focusing on my heartache, I try to fill the gaps with happiness and teach my girls that they are free to be beautiful people without needing to look after me. Because I was never free to grow and discover without the responsibility of caring for Mum when I became an adult, I want more than anything for my children to have that freedom.'

# Shazna's story

## 29 years old, From Australia

**On loss:**
'When I was 17, my mum was diagnosed with cancer. She was very ill for almost two years before she died. Watching her go through that pain was horrible.'

**On gains:**
'Some of the things I learned from losing Mum was that when she died, she did not take anything with her. She wasn't a woman with a lot of wealth and never got the opportunity to live in her own house. She didn't get to have all that she wanted in life. I don't live with big hopes, wanting this and that. I just live my life happily with what I have. I try to teach my boys about values and responsibilities and to become good humans. I try my best to teach them to be happy with what they have.

'I also learned that life isn't certain. We may be called at anytime. My mum's death made me much stronger and I learned to face difficulties on my own. Mental strength is very much needed! I thank God for not letting me drown and helping me to be stronger and face the world. When I look back and think, I am proud of what I have achieved. I am proud that I was able to manage everything on my own with both of my boys without any family support. I know my mum was a very strong person. I am glad that I have gained that from her.'

**On wishing:**

'If I ever had a day with my mum, I would tell her how much I love her and how much I adore her. When she was alive, I never said it to her and I regret that a lot.'

# Jodie's story

## 42 years old, From Australia

**On loss:**
'I lost my mum in 2010. She wasn't supposed to die. She was my mother. She was supposed to always be there for me, my one constant—but I lost that.

'The day my mum died, I left palliative care at about 6.30am. My sister came in so that I could go home and get some sleep. I got a phone call in the early afternoon to get back to the hospital. I didn't make it in time. My dear beautiful mother had died.

'Mum died surrounded by family and friends, but I wasn't there—I had missed her. That afternoon in hospital, I took her gold bangle off her wrist and placed it on mine. This is where it has stayed. That strong person I knew Mum to be had gone. Part of me went with her, I think. How do I live life without my mum? Losing my mum broke my heart.'

**On missing:**
'I miss not being able to pick up the phone and chat. Mum would always call me and we would talk about nothing. How I miss those phone calls.'

**On coping:**
'Having my own children helped me to get through Mum's death because I had to be strong for them. As a mother, you have to get up and still keep being a mum. Even though your world has been

shattered, the world for everyone else just keeps going.

'We still have a cake for "Nanny's birthday" and sing 'Happy Birthday' to her. We have lots of wonderful and funny memories that the kids love to recall about her. It makes us smile.

'I miss her like crazy but I feel her presence everywhere. I have had a few things happen since she passed and I just know that it is her. She never believed in any of that stuff but I am sure she does now. She gives me many signs and that gives me great comfort.'

# Tina's story

## 29 years old, From Australia

**On loss:**

'The day I lost my mum, I woke to my four sisters in my house. One of them had a key and they had let themselves in. They knew my husband was away and that I couldn't take this news alone. I started to shake and sob. I looked over to the bassinet beside me where my six-week old daughter lay sleeping. All I could say was, "But Mum hasn't met my little girl yet".

'My baby girl arrived four weeks early—a surprise to us all. Mum couldn't believe it had happened so early and so quickly. She was so thrilled to have a granddaughter after four grandsons.

'Following my daughter's birth, Mum called almost every day—mostly just to say "Hi", have a chat and check that we were doing ok. She would often remind me to make sure that my baby was warm. She told me of things she was planning to do, like make rice porridge with fish when we started solids and buy her granddaughter a gold bracelet when she went on her trip to Singapore. She proudly carried a little photo album with baby pictures of her granddaughter to share with everyone she knew.'

**On coping:**

'I try to be positive. My mum knew I'd had a beautiful, healthy baby girl. We got to do video calls and she got to see lots of photos. I got to speak to Mum almost every day in those first six weeks of my daughter's life and tell her about her amazing new granddaughter. I feel lucky that we had 'extra' time and not just the short time that we'd have had if my daughter had been born when she was due.'

# Tracey's story

## 32 years old, From Australia

**On loss:**

'I was 27 when I had my first child and I remember the excitement Mum felt at becoming a grandmother. She would light up at holding my daughter and enjoyed her immensely. She would often pop in with lunch for me and on the days she didn't visit, she would call—often very early, waking the whole house.

'The last time I saw my mum, she had called in after going to the supermarket. At the time, I was feeding my daughter who was four months old. Mum touched my daughter on the head with her hand and said she wouldn't kiss us because she felt like she was getting a cold. With that, she left. Two days later, Mum passed away suddenly.

'A coroner's report six months later would prove to be inconclusive. My mother, at 47 years of age, had gone without explanation—without the chance to say goodbye.

'Often the pain has been too much to bear and I think it will surely break me, then I cry. I still cry. I have missed out on so much and so has Mum. The shock of losing Mum is not something I think will ever leave me.'

**On coping:**

'We do not remember the days—we remember the moments. At the very moment that I lost Mum, I changed. As awful as this experience has been, it has made me stronger. It has made my family so much closer to each other. It has made me want to be a better person. I have learned to slow down and appreciate things. I have learned that a little kindness goes a long way, especially towards others.

'Nothing anyone can say or do can ease the pain, but during the dark days I feel Mum with me always. I am so incredibly proud of myself for picking up the pieces and making my life into something wonderful. I believe everything happens for a reason and the lessons we learn along the way shape who we are. Sometimes those lessons are painful, but sometimes we can turn them into something positive to share with those who love us most and those who we love more than anything in this world.'

**On wishing:**
'I never got the chance to say good-bye and I am not sure, if given the chance, that I could do it even now. How do you begin to say good-bye to someone who gave you everything they could offer? I would give anything to hear Mum's voice, to see her infectious smile, to hug her one more time and to be woken up by one more early morning phone call. I would tell her how much I appreciated her and how much she mattered to me. She was always there whenever I needed her and even at times when I thought that I didn't.'

# Angela's story

## 32 years old, From UK

**On loss:**

'From diagnosis to death, I had 11 months with my mum. Eleven months of watching her go from a young, able woman to a very thin, frail old lady. I can't cope with thinking about that. It tortures me to think that I could do nothing to cure her. I had to stand back and watch it happen—and now she's gone. I miss her more than I'm able to express.'

**On coping:**

'I think I stamp the pain down inside me. Or maybe I let it go, let it fly away. Every time it hurts really badly, I just have to 'cope' because my daughter needs me and now my newborn son needs me also. I have to be as good a mum as my own mum was.

'Keeping busy helps. I think of Mum fondly. I remember the good times. My auntie told me that each time you see a white feather it means an angel is near you. Well, I swear, I see white feathers all the time! I'm not looking for them, but I see them and I know Mum's there. She wants to be with us and that tears me apart. It makes me smile too, though, because I know at times that she's content just watching.'

**On wishing:**

'If I could spend one more day with my mum, I'd go back to when I was 15 years old or so and cut the woman some slack. I'd make dinner and tidy up afterwards. I'd make her a coffee and let her sit down. I'd stop asking for things. I'd tell her that if she didn't stop smoking, she'd die at 58 and not get to see her grandchildren grow up. I'd tell her I love her and give her a big hug (I did this all the time, but could do it forever).'

# Ann-Maree's story

## 23 years old, From UK

**On loss:**
'I lost my mother unexpectedly in January 2012 when she was 63 years of age. I was just shy of 22 years old. I fell pregnant seven months after my mother passed away. Knowing that I was going to be bringing a baby into the world without my mum was the scariest thing to me. I thought I wouldn't be able to do it without her. I almost felt as if I needed her to supervise me being a parent. It upsets me that I was never able to share with her the news about expecting and the baby's sex or take her along with me to visits with my obstetrician.'

**On wishing:**
'Sometimes I feel denied and lost because my mum isn't around. Sometimes I even envy others who still have their mums and can rely on them for help.

'When I found out that I was pregnant, I just wanted my mum. I wanted her to be there with me, to tell me it was going to be ok and to help me deal with all the crazy emotions that had started to consume me. To this day, I always wonder what she would think of me as a mother—whether she'd be proud of me. I also wonder what it would be like to just have her around when things get tough and I need an extra hand or support.'

# Emily's story

## 31 years old, From Australia

**On loss:**

'I lost my mum to cancer in 1996. I was 14 years old and she was 42. We never, ever saw Mum give up hope. She continued to be a mother right up until the end.

'Losing Mum to cancer at 14 was awful. Fourteen isn't the most pleasant of ages and I was no exception. I didn't realise that I had so many questions that I needed answered before she left. It was as an adult that I realised what I'd really lost. I had lost the wisdom that a mum provides her child to help them navigate through life. There have been significant moments in my life when I needed Mum—a gentle hand to push me in the right direction or to pull me back when I was a lost soul.'

**On coping:**

'Although Mum never sat me down and left me with particular advice on parenting or life, I live every day by the moral compass that she instilled in me as a child. I know that I will pass this onto my children too.

'My baby daughter inherited my eyes. Those eyes that Mum gave me. Every time I look into my son's and daughter's eyes, I see my Mum and I realise that she will never leave me.'

**On wishing:**
'If I could spend one day with my mum, I wouldn't say anything. I would just sit with her, hold her hand and breathe in her energy and spirit. I would give anything to be with her for one more day and watch the world go by.'

# Sally's story

## 42 years old, From UK

**On loss:**
'I lost my mum when I was 19 years old. Mum had been diagnosed with breast cancer when I was 10. When I was 16, she had a mastectomy and I took over as her principle personal carer at home. She needed help in the shower, for example. As a mum myself now, I can only imagine what strength it took her to accept help from her 16 year old daughter. My beautiful, wonderful mum lost her fight in 1989.

Mum's illness and death made me grow up very fast.'

**On missing:**
'The first time I realised the enormity of the hole that she had left in my life was when I was pregnant for the first time in 2004. I needed my mum. For the first time since she had left me, I couldn't do it on my own.

'The next time I missed my Mum to such a degree was when I was pregnant again, with my twins in 2007. I had an absolutely awful time of it. I just needed her to be there to look after me and tell me that it was going to be all right.

'When my twins arrived, my whole world seemed to turn upside down. I was jealous of other mums with twins who had their own mums to help them out. I had never really felt jealous about others having their mothers around before, but now I did. And then I had the most terrible guilt about feeling jealous—I wondered if this jealousy made me a terrible person.'

**On coping:**

'I do believe that not having a mum for so long has shaped me into a strong and independent woman. I have no way of knowing whether I would be a different type of mum were my own mum still alive. Probably not. I miss her terribly, but I've always just got on with it—what other choice is there?'

# Liselle's story

## 32 years old, From Australia

**On loss:**
'My mum died aged 63. I was 31 years old. Mum was diagnosed with advanced dementia in late 2006. She rapidly deteriorated. On most of the occasions when I got home from visiting her, I would vomit numerous times from the stress and shock of the visit. So, for self-preservation, I often couldn't visit her.

'To me, during this time, although my mum was physically alive, she was merely a shell of someone who resembled my mum. Her mind and soul had died many years ago. Everybody deals with situations differently and now I understand what this means. I loved Mum every one of those days that she was on this earth and I still do. I miss her more than words can describe. Not a day went by while she was struggling that I didn't have at least one conversation in my head with her and I still do, everyday.'

**On coping:**
'A mother is a reinforcer. She has travelled the road you are travelling and knows that the goal is getting to the end with the least injuries to all involved! A mother is able to be honest without leaving you feeling as though you've been judged. A mother will be supportive while keeping you grounded. Being a mother without a mum is a bit like walking blindfolded. You don't know what lies ahead and when you get there, you have to push through on the advice of others who really know

nothing intimate about you, your life or what you have been through. You don't share that maternal bond or trust with these others, yet their advice is all you have to go on.'

**On missing:**
'Probably one of the first times that Mum's illness hit me hard was when I told her that I was pregnant. She had been suffering from advanced dementia for two years and could no longer talk or recognise anyone or anything. Did she understand anything I was saying? I'll never know, but I like to think so.

'When your baby is born, there are those two days of euphoria then reality hits with a thud. There are all those questions you want to ask, all those things you want to know, all those emotions that make you feel you're possibly going crazy—or perhaps is it just lack of sleep. In those times, no-one seems to understand you like your mum.

'I wish that Mum could have shared time with my kids. Those nights where she would have loved to take them for a movie and a sleepover and spoil them rotten. I know in my heart that she would have been someone they would have listened to and pushed the limit with but never crossed the line. She was the one who would always know what to do in any situation and would follow things through to the end. I miss not having that comfort in my life.'

**On wishing:**
'Mum taught me that all you really need to be a good mother is love, stability and positivity and even without her, I can pass that onto my kids. Oh, but what I wouldn't give to say "Mum" and get an answer.'

# Jo's story

## 38 years old, From UK

**On loss:**
'I remember the painful day when my mum died far too clearly. It was six years ago, before my two little boys were so much as a thought. I will always remember the shock, confusion and emptiness of that day and of so many days, months and years that followed. I don't believe that you ever recover from this kind of loss. Instead, you learn to adapt and in your own way, to accept it.'

**On coping:**
'Over time, I realised that I didn't need to look down upon a concrete plaque to feel a connection and closeness to my mum. She was there all the time, immersing herself in all of our lives. She was there within our family home, watching out for her grandsons just like grandmothers do.'

# Joanna's story

### 39 years old, From UK

**On loss:**
'I lost my mum when I was 26 years old. It was a shock, as she was only 49 and from diagnosis to death, it was only six weeks. There is no way that I thought I would cope with such a heartbreaking loss.'

**On coping:**
'The way I honour my mum is to make sure that I remain positive and happy and enjoy my life to the full. I know she would have wanted this for me more than anything else. It's only now, as I've become a mother myself, that I truly know and understand this. My boys are my world and if I had only one wish for them, it would be happiness.

'Mum taught me: to never judge another; to look for the hidden beauty in everything; to enjoy times of solitude; to feel empowered to do things alone; to travel and see as much of the world as possible; to avoid the material aspects of life, but to enjoy quality; to be independent and to always find the positive.'

**On wishing:**
'If I had one day with my mum, it would be spent with her and my boys. We would make play dough and set out treasure hunts around the garden. We would eat her homemade lasagna and just be. I would tell her how grateful I am for the childhood she gave me and for the person who I've become. I would hold her.'

# Veronica's story

## 32 years old, From Australia

**On loss:**

'When I lost my mother, I was 17 years old and had a 14 year old sister. Mum died of lung cancer, which was not related to smoking. She was diagnosed just after I had turned 16 and within 12 months, she had passed away.

'When Mum got sick, she was ready to fight it with everything she had. Chemo knocked her around as it does to everyone. She drank that much carrot juice that she started to turn orange. She really did give it her best shot. Meanwhile, I was working two jobs, looking after my sister, trying to run a household—juggling bills, cleaning and more— and trying to visit Mum as often as I could get there. Eventually it all became too much for me. I quit my jobs to spend more time with Mum.

'I went to see Mum one Friday and told her that I was going to spend a week with Dad. She was barely conscience anymore, due to the pain relief and she could only eat this thick liquid. When I left that day, I bent down and gave her a kiss on her forehead, told her that I loved her and that I'd see her when I got back.

'Late Saturday evening, I was lying in bed talking with Dad and the phone rang. I just knew. I heard Dad talking and knew that I was right. She had gone. I think I was crying before he even came back to let me know. Two days after her birthday and when my sister and I were both with people who loved us and would look after us, Mum passed away in her sleep.'

**On coping:**

'Losing Mum changed my view on life. I know how quickly life can be taken away and how easily it can change.

'Family is important to me, above everything else. I had to grow up really fast and because of my experiences when Mum was sick, I am open and honest with my children—even if it may not be what they really want to hear or could be upsetting to them. I am realistic yet caring and considerate of my children. We trust each other. We can talk with each other. I don't hold secrets from them. We are honest.'

# Kym's story

## 29 years old, From Australia

**On loss:**
'My mum got sick when I was around seven years old. After seven years of being chronically ill, spending months at a time in and out of hospital, undergoing countless operations and a double lung transplant, Mum passed away from renal failure in 1999.

'I have one younger brother and two older brothers. I remember thinking, as we walked out of the hospital that final time, that I was now responsible for these boys. At 14 years old, I suddenly became "mum" to my brothers.'

**On coping:**
'Looking back, I see how much my mum put into her fight to live, to be around to watch my brothers and I grow up a little more each day. She missed so much of our growing up—all out of her control, due to illness—that this has made me that much more present in my own children's lives. If there's an assembly at school, a dance, sports days, T-ball games or anything like that, I move heaven and earth to be there so that my kids have their mum around.'

**On wishing:**
'If I could spend one more day with my mum, I'd love her to meet my wonderful hubby. I'd want her to see my nine year old daughter dance, watch my eight year old son play T-ball, see my six year old do

cartwheels and read, play with my four and one year olds. By far my kids are my greatest achievement, which is funny because I know she felt the same way about my brothers and I.'

# Jette's story
## 34 years old, From Germany

**On loss:**
'I lost my mum to ovarian cancer when I was 28 years old. I gave birth to my own daughter 585 days after Mum's death. My husband and I named our daughter after my mum. We wanted to honour her that way.'

**On missing:**
'Becoming a mother is the most challenging, overwhelming experience that any woman can have. I have never missed Mum more than in those life-changing first weeks of new motherhood.

'Mum and I were quite close. I never doubted for a second that I was truly and completely loved by my mum and I knew that I could always rely on her. This is something that I cherish and is a gift that I hope to pass onto my children.

'I remember sitting at my mum's bedside when she was already weakened by her illness. At one point I told her, in tears, that I wasn't sure I could raise kids without her advice. She, also in tears, replied that I'd make a fine mum but that she was so sorry that she couldn't see her grandchild growing up. She'd always dreamed of being a granny.'

**On coping:**
'I learned so much from Mum and my parents provided me with everything I needed to be the best mum I can be. It strikes me how many

things that were important to my mother are also important to me, like meals shared as a family or doing stuff for my kids.

'My daughter is now three years old and we've already had the first chances to talk about my mum. I hope that one day she'll be able to say, "I never met my grandmother, but I bear her name and I'm proud of it".'

# Michelle's story

## 32 years old, From Australia

**On loss:**
'I lost my mum just after my 25<sup>th</sup> birthday. She was my best friend and I talked to her daily.

'Mum was taken from us suddenly, by a heart attack. In the early hours of the morning, Mum was sitting at the kitchen table and had a heart attack in front of my four younger siblings, the youngest being six years old. I remember getting a call from my dad. He said, "Mum isn't well. Come to the hospital". A nurse met me in the car park and took me into a room where my dad and siblings were. The words that came out of Dad's mouth changed our lives forever. "Your mum didn't make it," he said.

'We were told we could go and see her. She looked so peaceful laying there holding a white rose. That picture is etched into my mind. My best friend was gone.

'Mum passed away in December 2005, so the first Christmas without her was horrible. We tried to make it special for the young ones, but it was still tough.'

**On missing:**
'I met my husband in the March after Mum's passing. It was a welcome distraction from my heartache. We got married two years later. After a few months, we fell pregnant and the one person who I wanted to tell wasn't around anymore. I had so many questions that only Mum

could answer.'

'In January 2009, our little man was born. My heart yearned for my mum. I wanted her there—I needed her to teach me what to do. I wanted her to meet her first grandchild that she had always so looked forward to.'

# Helen's story

## 37 years old, From UK

**On missing:**
'I miss Mum the most when I read an incredible book or when I hear music that I know she'd love. I celebrate a small success and know that no-one celebrates your successes with you quite like your mum. The main thing I've learned is that not so many people truly appreciate their mums until they're gone.'

**On coping:**
'I think about what an amazing mum I had. Some never have the experience of having an amazing mum, or even having any mum at all. I have to be thankful that I had Mum in my life for as long as I did.

'I read my son poems that my mum read me, play him music that Mum listened to, repeat sayings that she had and cook meals that she cooked. I know that these things will instill a sense of who she was and of the positivity she had.

'Losing my mum made me consciously go back and remember all the very best memories of our time together. I revisit these memories in a way that I didn't while she was here. This can bring so much happiness.'

# Tamara's story

## 32 years old, From Australia

**On loss:**
'My mum passed away when I was nearly 10 years old. She had battled lung cancer for quite a few months and was told she was in remission. A few weeks later, she became unwell and was taken to hospital during the night. She never came home and I still don't really understand what happened.

'After Mum died, it was just my dad and I. He had no idea what to do and I remember very clearly, Dad burning the steak and chips he was trying to cook for dinner not long after she'd passed. So I stepped up. I became chief cook, cleaner and bill payer.'

**On coping:**
'I developed a sense of independence and of having to stand on my own two feet. This has served me well in a lot of situations—I've lived alone, I've travelled alone, and I've put myself through university.

'I deal with the loss by living one day at a time, knowing that tomorrow gives me new opportunities to experience life and that I need to keep positive for positive things to happen.'

**On wishing:**
'If I could spend one more day with my mum, I would talk endlessly, ask a million questions, watch her play with my daughters, introduce her to my husband, touch her, smell her, cook with her—a day wouldn't be enough!'

# Kim's story

## 41 years old, From Australia

**On loss:**
'My mother died 10 years ago. She fought a terrific battle with cancer—like so many do—and finally succumbed in August 2003. Mum passed away five years before I met my husband and well before we created our daughter, her granddaughter, in October 2013.'

**On missing**
'My daughter won't know her grandmother. At times this makes me incredibly sad. I've felt this sadness particularly in the early days of my pregnancy and in recent months as I nurse my perfect newborn daughter. With all those helpful hormones running riot inside me, I've found myself crying more for my mother since the birth of my baby than during the time of Mum's actual passing. I think that, at the time, I was too busy being angry at the world that she was dying! But amidst all the tears and longing ache for my mother, something wonderful has happened. I've realised just how much my mother has left behind her for my daughter and I.'

**On coping:**
'My mother taught me to be practical. This has seeded a common sense and a calm approach to newborn baby conundrums which, I'm certain, have helped me manage being a new mother at 41 years old.

'I find that my mother's tenderness in times of emotional upset has also taken root in me. She used to call my sister and I "darling heart" as a term of endearment. Not long after my daughter was born, I found myself reaching for the right words to soothe her. Without consciously being aware of it, I began calling her "darling heart". It wasn't until my husband mentioned how lovely the term sounded that I had to think about its origin.

'So many of my mannerisms and life skills originated during the 31 years that I had my mother here beside me, that I don't truly feel like a motherless mother. Sure, she may not be at the end of the phone or actually here to help me negotiate this whole new world of my new baby, but I hear her words of wisdom whispering in my ear from time to time. She tells me to stay calm and listen to my baby. I see her pause to reflect on the wonderment that is the new life I have created. It makes me slow down and reflect myself.

'The thought of how Mum would interact with and love her grand-daughter makes me smile. I miss her every day, especially now, but it's true what they say—loved ones don't ever really leave you, they are always beside you: in the lessons you learned from them; the stories they shared with you; and the memories you keep.'

# Elke's story

## 32 years old, From Belgium

**On loss:**
'In August 2012, when I had just returned from a weekend with our friends in London, we received the worst phone call ever. My dad phoned from France, where he was on holiday with my mom, to tell us she had passed away a couple of hours ago. It was very unexpected.'

**On missing:**
'While I was pregnant, I missed being able to ask Mom the questions that I had about things being 'normal' or not. Now that I'm a mother, I even miss her more. I think having your own children brings you to the realisation and understanding of how your mom felt about you, being her child. That experience is something I would've wanted to talk about with her.'

**On coping:**
'The pain is better now after such a long time. Things that I have difficulties with include beautiful music, especially music that I listened to when she was still alive. Sometimes, when I'm having a 'down' day, I get tears in my eyes when I see grandmothers walking around with their grandchildren or when I see commercials about grandparents and grandchildren.

'I deal with it by talking with my husband or friends, or just letting the tears come. Sometimes I have to cry when the pain is too much.

After crying, I usually feel 'lighter'.

**On wishing:**
'If I could spend one more day with my mom, I think that I would tell her how much I love her and how much I appreciate everything she did for me and for my husband. I sometimes feel that I didn't say that enough when she was here. We knew how we felt, but it wasn't said a lot. But then again, if it was just one day then I would maybe do nothing but enjoy each other's company at home with a cup of tea and a nice cake and talk about everything, about happy things. It's something that I daydream about.'

# Catherine's story
## 36 years old, From Australia

**On missing:**
'My mum passed away unexpectedly when I was 17. I think the first time that I fully understood the sadness of not having my mum around was during the planning of my wedding, 10 years after she died. Not having her there to help me pick my dress, not having her there to be so excited for me and to love my husband the way I know she would have loved him. It felt quite unbearable at times.

   'The next time I truly understood just how much I longed to have my mum around was definitely when I found out that I was going to become a mum myself. I had so many unanswered questions and so many fears about the pregnancy, the labour and then raising the baby. I felt like I was ripped off again: deprived of that safety blanket that comes with having the baby's grandma around; lacking the reassurance that if you stuff up, your mum will help you fix it; or having your mum there just to cuddle you or the baby and help you know that everything will be all right.'

**On coping:**
'I know my life would be so different if my mum was still here. I still might have ended up in the same place, but I think the journey would have been very different. I was not a person to be very proud of back then and although I lost my mum, the shock gave me perspective on becoming a good person that I think would have taken many more

years to gain. It didn't happen straight away, but I think I grew up quickly and made it my mission to become the type of person that Mum would have been proud of.'

**On wishing:**
'If I could spend one day with my mum again, I would definitely spend it by introducing her to my husband and son. I know my mum had a say in me choosing him, even though she wasn't there. I knew he was right for me because I knew she would love him.

'I definitely know that my son is the beautiful boy that he is because of the person Mum made me through her own mothering and guidance. I feel like I'm a lot like my mum and if that is truly so, then I must be a good person, a loyal friend and a great mum. I would love to get the opportunity to tell her that and of course, just thank her for everything she helped to create in my life. I'd tell her that she still continues to help mould my life, even though she's not here.'

# Eloise's story

## 36 years old, From Australia

**On loss:**
'My mother passed away at 57 years of age. It was cancer that took her from us, in a cruel and tormented way. I was 27 at the time. I never understood the saying 'heavy heart', but now I do. It literally felt like my heart was the heaviest part of my body and it hurt, a lot.'

**On coping:**
'Life went on and I got married, then fell pregnant. My pregnancy happened quicker than we expected and we were very happy to be bringing a new life into our family. I fretted and worried as most first-timers do, but generally enjoyed my 42 weeks (yes 42 weeks!) of pregnancy.

'I'd always assumed that my mother would be there for the birth of my children—literally there, in the delivery suite I mean. Giving birth terrified me. We hired a doula, which for me offered the best peace of mind and was the closest thing to having a maternal presence there for me during childbirth. Our doula was motherly, tender and simply beautiful to both my husband and I.'

**On missing:**
'I can't hide it—I am jealous of other mothers in the company of their mothers. They are everywhere: cafes, supermarkets, parks and street corners. You name it and they are there, enjoying each other's company

in the presence of a child. I feel lonely, ripped off, angry and mostly, heartbroken for my son who will never get to meet his grandma.'

# Charlie's story

## 38 years old, From UK

**On loss:**
'My mum died of cervical cancer 25 years ago, when I was 12 years old. I lost my mum when I was so young that I feel I missed out on the friend bit, that woman-to-woman relationship that I see my friends have with their mums. That makes my heart ache.'

**On missing:**
'I felt the loss of my mum the hardest when I became a mum. The pride, the fear and the heart-bursting love you feel when you hold your child—that's when I needed her the most.

'As my babies grew, my grief and my loss seemed to change. It shifted from the longing and yearning to have Mum there to being brokenhearted over how she must have felt, knowing that she was dying.'

**On wishing:**
'I would have given anything for my mum to be around when I had my daughter. I was so scared. Scared about whether I was going to be enough for my daughter, whether I was a good mum. It's been a learning curve for the two of us.'

# Raychelle's story

## 35 years old, From Australia

**On loss:**

'My mum passed away in 2011. She suffered from and ultimately lost a battle with Alzheimer's Disease. I found that while my heart ached upon the loss of Mum, we had, in truth, been mourning her for many years beforehand as she wilted away from this terrible, unfair disease.'

**On missing:**

'My mum was the most amazing, caring, beautiful, bright, loving woman that I have ever met and will ever be lucky enough to meet. She loved me unconditionally and was always there for me when I needed her.

'I was lucky enough to have a mother who I could trust completely, who I could speak to about anything at any time of the day. If she was busy, she would stop for us. If she was at work, she would down tools and listen. She was my best friend. I miss her dearly every single day and would give anything to have her back again so that my sons could experience her love and adoration.'

# Jane's story

## 31 years old, From USA

**On loss:**
'My mother passed away when my first child was only four months old. I was not able to attend the funeral because I already lived in the USA, but I was able to fly to Moscow later on to spend time with my sister.

'I regret that my mom never got to hold her grandchildren. I regret that my children never knew their Russian grandmother—she would have been a sweet and caring one. No matter how tough her life may have been, there is something about a Russian grandmother's sweetness toward her grandchildren. So it brings me to tears to have that element missing from my own family. I miss my mom and I wish the latter years of her life could have been filled with her sweet grandchildren: their hugs and kisses, their unconditional love and their silliness.'

**On coping:**
'Being a young mother without the help or support of my own mom made me look for it elsewhere. I was blessed with a best friend, a woman 10 years my senior. I am thankful for this wonderful role model. I believe it is important for women, moms, to cultivate deep, meaningful friendships that go beyond park play dates and diaper brand talks. Only when you are a mother will you understand another mom's struggle or be able to share her joy in the way that she hopes to share in yours too.'

**On gains:**

'When I look at where I am at, as a motherless mother, I do not want my mind to dwell on the loss or sadness of the thought. I want to use it as motivation and have a vision for my relationship with my daughter and my sons. I want to create those special memories with them. I want to take time to hug and kiss them until they beg "No more!". I want to have that sincere connection with my children and show them that I am always here for them, no matter what.'

# Lisa's story

## 38 years old, From Australia

**On loss:**
'On the weekend over which my world changed forever, Mum and I had gone to Melbourne for my niece's first birthday. On the way there, my mum said that she felt cold and she was rubbing her left arm while driving. We made it to my sister's place and Mum walked in the door, greeted the babies then said, "Thank god we're here". That was the last thing she said to any of us. Mum then collapsed and unbeknownst to us, was having a massive heart attack. My two sisters were there and were amazing. They performed CPR until the ambulances came. I was going crazy, shaking uncontrollably and panicking. I knew deep down that something sinister was happening.

'Mum was rushed to hospital. My dad was called and brought down to Melbourne by family friends. Two days later, the day before my 18th birthday, my beautiful mum was declared brain dead. It was one of the hardest days of my life.'

**On missing:**
'We consider ourselves to be so lucky to have this opportunity to provide our beautiful children, now aged nine and seven, with a loving stable home. It breaks my heart, though, that they will not get to: feel the love of their grandparents; spend time with them at their house; go the shop to buy ice creams; or have them come to school on 'Grandparents Day'. I find that I can get randomly emotional at school or

dance concerts, or even at Christmas carols, when I look around the room and see all of the other grandparents there, smiling and proud as punch of their grandchild. My heart wrenches. I have had to pull myself together, stuck in the middle of an audience, sobbing my heart out. I see other kids with their grandparents and wonder how that makes my children feel. I can only hope their pain is not as much as my own.'

# Sarah's story

## 26 years old, From UK

**On loss:**

'I was 22 years old when I lost my mum. When I think back to the day of her death, I just feel angry. She died alone in a hospital and I felt that I had let her down.

'When I was seven, Mum was diagnosed with non-Hodgkin's lymphoma and went through various treatments. Christmas 2004 hit us with something else. Mum complained of a headache throughout Christmas Day and when she woke up on Boxing Day, she fell over. I woke to a doctor being called to the house, where we were told she'd suffered a mini stroke and had to be taken to hospital.

'Mum left hospital the following day with a slight limp and was told to rest. Being a typical mother though, she didn't completely rest and on New Years Eve she went to feed the cat. This is when she suffered another mini stroke, but this time she lost mobility for a short time and couldn't talk.

'Many years later in August 2008, just after I turned 21, Mum had two mini strokes again while she was in a London hospital. At this time, I was working full time as a nursery nurse. Following Mum's two mini strokes, we decided as a family that I would quit my job and be her carer from 8.30am–6.00pm every day. I fed Mum, washed her, changed her and made sure she was getting the correct medication.

'The day before Mum died, she slept all day. I sat there and watched her sleep, trying to wake her to eat—but I had no luck. At 8.00am the following day, I answered a phone call from the hospital telling me to get to there immediately as my mum was very ill. I raced there and was told on arrival that Mum had died around 9.00am. Her blood pressure had dropped so low that her heart had stopped. They had resuscitated her but it hasn't lasted long.

'When Mum died, I was around six weeks pregnant.'

**On coping:**
'I just cope. I have to. I have a son that I need to take care of, so I have to be strong. I'm the one who my sister and my dad talk to if they miss Mum. I'm the one who cleaned the house and held us together every time Mum was in hospital. I feel that I have to be strong for everyone. I miss Mum everyday. I talk about her to my son all the time. He knows she's a star in the sky and will point her out whenever he sees stars! I need to keep her memory alive so that my son knows what a wonderful woman she was.'

# Lilla's story
## 49 years old, From Australia

**On loss:**

'In 2001, my mother was walking through Martin Place in Sydney when a gentleman stopped her and said, "You really should see someone about that mole on your shoulder". The mass was removed and it was a melanoma.

'During the period of time from November 2006 to July 2007, my mother's health deteriorated rapidly. With the support of my husband, I cared for her. It was heartbreaking but at the same time, so many things were discussed and so much love shared. For the first time ever, I didn't care about anyone or anything else other than my dying mother. I ignored my beautiful daughter and my supportive, loving husband—they were no longer my priority.

'In July 2007, my mother flew to Switzerland with my step-dad and was euthanised. She was aged 64 and I was 43. What a brave, amazing woman to be able to make such a decision and to die with dignity.'

**On missing:**

'After Mum passed, I was emotionally numb. I cried each and every day for years and I had an enormous sense of guilt that I didn't travel with her to Switzerland. I still regret my decision to this day. It's not OK that she is no longer with me. We used talk daily on the phone about nothing in particular—sometimes more than once a day. Even now, six years have passed and I miss our daily telephone chats, I miss her presence and I miss having somebody to nurture me like only a mother can.'

**On wishing:**

'If I could spend just one more day with my mother, we would: watch the sun rise over North Bondi; swim in the ocean; share oysters and wine in the David Jones food hall at Bondi Junction; and talk and laugh together. I would hug and kiss her and tell her how much I love, adore and respect her. I would tell her again what a wonderful mother and grandmother she is, how much she is loved, that I miss her and that I will always have a hole in my heart that will never be filled. We would cook together, drink wine and simply enjoy each and every precious moment.'

# Suzi's story

## 28 years old, From Australia

**On loss:**
'I was only in primary school when my mother first got sick. She was diagnosed with breast cancer and being young, I didn't know what that meant but I knew it was bad. I remember it being a tough time for Mum, going through chemotherapy and even a mastectomy, but thankfully she managed to pull through. Little did we know, however, that the cancer would come back years later.

'When the cancer returned, it attacked Mum's lungs and was a lot more aggressive. At this point I was in high school and I was more aware of what was going on. I wasn't even 14 years old when my mother passed away. It was so unbelievably hard on me at the time, but I had no idea how hard it was going to get as time went on.'

**On missing:**
'I struggled with not having my mum the most when I was pregnant for the first time. I cried so much about the fact that I didn't have my mum to ask for advice and to go to for help. Knowing that she would never get to meet my child, nor would my baby ever get to know her, was so painful. I now have two beautiful girls, a two year old and an almost five month old—and I still cry for my mum.'

**On coping:**

'I can definitely see differences in my parenting compared to my friends who still have their mothers. I see how close they are to their mums and how much they rely on them. I see how, since having children themselves, they seem to have become closer 'friends' with their mothers. Not having this myself is hard, especially when I see others' closeness with their mums. I guess I just try to focus on my relationship with my girls and ensure that they, at least, have that if I can't.

'Being without my mum has definitely made me more independent too. I don't like to rely on others and feel like, "I can do this myself. There's no reason why I can't". It's made me a stronger person.

'I never got the chance to say goodbye to my mother. I know that she knew that I loved her, but I wish I had said it that one last time. I now make sure that I say "I love you" to my girls as much as I can. Losing my mother has made me truly appreciate life and how precious and short it really is.'

# Kristin's story

## 32 years old, From Australia

**On loss:**
'My mum was diagnosed with multiple sclerosis (MS) when I was about seven or eight. At that age, I didn't really understand as there were no obvious signs of the disease. As I got into my teens, though, Mum was gradually getting worse. I was angry about this and almost resented her for it. I feel terrible for even saying that. I wanted my mum to be normal, like everyone else's.

'I went to university at age 18 and lived away from home for three years. In that time, Mum really got worse.

'I fell pregnant at age 21 while at university. After I finished my Law degree, I moved back to my hometown. Mum was still able to hold my baby girl, but not for long. I lived five minutes away so, on the days I didn't work, I would be with Mum and my daughter.

'When my daughter was about three or four years old, my mum started to lose her mind due to the MS. She had to have 24-hour care and was put into a nursing home. This is when I probably needed her the most. I could no longer ring up and ask her a quick question.

'The day Mum didn't recognise me was the day I thought I had lost my mum. At the time of her actual death, though, it felt like the greatest shock of all and I couldn't cope for the first few weeks.'

**On wishing:**
'If Mum could be here just for one day, I would want her to spend it with my children—playing with them, spoiling them, just being with them. I think I've learnt to cope by myself, I just wish she were here for my children more so than for me. I wish that she could see them grow up and for them to see how loved they are by her.'

# Kristie's story

## 33 years old, From Australia

**On loss:**
'My mum died of cancer in July 2011. It was brutal and sudden. 'Stage four' are two of the worst words in existence, because as we all know there is no 'stage five'. We never saw it coming, there was no warning and there was no time. That, I think, was the most awful thing. No time. No time for denial. No time for anger. Just skip right to acceptance. My mum touched so many lives that it is such a waste—a travesty—that when I need her the most, she's not here.'

**On missing:**
'The thing I miss the most is time. You never get it in advance and can never get it back. I wanted my mum to have more special times. I wanted to share my daughter's achievements with Mum and let her see me bringing up a small version of myself. I wanted to hear her say, "That was just like you when you were little". I miss having someone to bounce questions off. Other mums like me are trying to figure it out, but grandmothers have done it.'

**On coping:**
'The truth is there is no time left, only memories. I can choose to be sad that my daughter will miss sharing all of these things with Mum or I can make it my mission to ensure my mum is remembered through the things I do with my daughter. The way I cope is by teaching my

daughter the things I wanted my mum to teach her. We cook, we laugh, I read to her about crystals (my mum's passion was crystal healing), we do things and go places that I know my mum would have wanted to take my daughter to. I choose to try and honour my mum in all the things I do with my daughter.'

**On gains:**

'This loss has defined how I parent and who I am as a person. It has forced me to be my own support. Because just as much as my mum shaped who I am, her death made me realise that life is just way too short not to do the things that define a life: be engaged; go on holidays; passionately love the work that you do; listen; hold those moments in your heart every day. Every day, I live for the life that Mum didn't get. I capture the moments that she'll never see because she deserves to know that, even though she's not physically here, someone is marking the moments for her.'

# Kayt's story

## 42 years old, From UK

**On loss:**

'My mother was diagnosed with lung cancer a few months after my now-husband and I became engaged. On one hand, her suffering was quick and I was given the opportunity to say goodbye—although to this day, I still don't remember what I said and whether it was enough.'

'Mum passed away six days after my husband and I got married. We'd brought the wedding forward so that she could enjoy the day with us. I still remember Mum asking, when we arrived, whether we were really going to get married. She lived in South Africa and I lived in the UK.

'For me, my biggest fear had always been of losing my mum and life has a funny way of throwing your fears straight at you. I was 32 years old, newly married and I struggled. My goodness I struggled. I withdrew from my husband and friends and hated everyone who had a family and a mum. My dad has been absent for pretty much all of my life, so my mum was hugely important to me.'

**On gains:**

'Now, ten years on, I have realised that my mum gave me incredible strength as I have coped with so much since she died: death; IVF treatment; miracle baby number two; career highs; troubled marriage; and post natal depression. I was honoured to have had her influence in my life.

'Unfortunately my mum never met my two amazing children, but she lives in them. They have her spirit, humour and strength.

'When the going gets tough, I often think about what Mum would do and how she would handle a situation. I do remind myself as often as I can that nobody knows what's coming tomorrow, so I try not to sweat the small stuff and just enjoy these magical children who I never thought I would have.'

**On coping:**
'In the beginning, it was very tough as I didn't believe it was ok to be without Mum in my life. As time goes on, though, I remind myself that she gave me strength and got me to face my greatest fear—her death.

'I have also learnt to trust my instincts more without Mum here, as I cannot ask her if something I am doing is wrong or right. I have to go with my gut instead.'

# Skye's story

## 40 years old, From Australia

**On loss:**
'My mum died, somewhat unexpectedly, six years ago. She was 58 years old and I was 33. She died of a stroke.

'One morning, the alarm went off and I felt my husband get out of bed—but he didn't turn the alarm off and it kept ringing, waking me up more than I liked. Somewhere in that sleep/wake stage, I realised that it wasn't the alarm but the phone and my husband had got up to answer it. The ringing stopped just before he made it, but quickly started back up again. I looked at the clock—it was 2.00am. An involuntary chill went through me, but the practical side of my brain argued that it could be anything. I heard my husband say, "No, this is her husband. Hang on, I'll get her". I came down the hallway to the kitchen and listened to a doctor with an accent tell me that Mum had had a stroke, a bleed in the brain. She was being transferred to another hospital, on life support, for emergency surgery. Her condition was critical and I needed to come immediately.

'I am a nurse and an incredibly rational person, so the medically trained rational side of my brain took over. I considered: how had Mum been brought to hospital; who called for help; why wasn't I called earlier as she had been at the hospital for almost two hours. The answers I got didn't make sense to me. I didn't know if it was the doctor's accent, my brain or both. While I ran all these questions through my head, we rushed to the hospital and were soon allowed to see Mum.

'Mum was on life support, with a bandage covering her head from the surgery. In between calling family, I sat by her bed and cried and held her hand. I sat holding her hand and studying it, trying to commit every line, every wrinkle, to memory for all eternity. I thought to myself, "This is the very last time I will ever be with my mother while she is alive. This is the last time I will ever hold her hand while it is pink and warm". Eventually, Mum's body slowed and she passed quietly with me beside her, holding her hand for that final time.'

# Cassie's story

## 30 years old, From Australia

**On loss:**
'My mother was killed in a car accident in 2008 at the age of 53. I was 24 years old at the time. The night after the accident, I remember falling asleep on the lounge room floor at my parents' house thinking, "This is the first night I have spent in this world without my mum". It was the most surreal feeling—mostly shock I guess.'

**On missing:**
'I gave birth in 2010, two years after my mum died. In the beginning, it was unbearable some nights as I wished I could just pick up a phone and talk to her. She'd had four children. She was a fantastic mother, a real mother. I saw her parenthood ups and downs and all I wanted to do was share my own with her. I wanted her to know that I finally understood what it was like. Silence is deafening.'

**On coping:**
'Time heals. It has almost been five years since Mum passed and I am making it. We are surviving. My child is growing. My mother would be so proud. I smile when I imagine her face if she were to see all my little family has become. Time has definitely healed some of the pain.'

# Kristine's story

## 34 years old, From Australia

**On loss:**

'In 1996, I was in the prime of my angst-ridden, boy-crazy, grunge-loving, selfish, rude and lazy teenage years. My mum was sick, from what nobody could ascertain, but I was pretty disinterested because I had stuff to do: cigarettes to smoke and parties to go to. When the doctors finally established that it was cancer I was relieved because it meant she would go to hospital, get fixed and stop dry-retching in the toilet every day.

'Nobody told me it was one of those *really* bad cancers—pancreatic cancer that has a five per cent survival rate. So I went about my indulgent life, visiting Mum a grand total of three times in the six weeks that she was in hospital. Then, on 7 January 1997, I was dragged to Mum's bedside to say goodbye. I went in and said goodbye to someone I barely recognised, then she passed away.

'As a pretty immature 17 year old, I was way out of my emotional depth. I muddled through my final year of high school with average marks, but a certificate nonetheless. It was the first time I'd done something that I thought Mum would've been proud of—and it stung.'

**On missing:**

'Getting into university, graduating from university, going out with nice guys, breaking up with idiot guys, visiting the world, buying a house, getting married and of course, becoming a mother. These are some of the big ticket items in my life that I'm sure Mum would've loved—none more so than getting to know my husband and our two boys.'

# Chelsea's story

## 34 years old, From Australia

**On loss:**
'When Mum was diagnosed with stage four ovarian cancer, the doctors basically told her to go home and die—that there was nothing more they could do. I cannot describe to you the heartbreak I felt when Dad called me with this news, there are just no words to explain it.

'I eventually got the call from Dad that I was dreading but knew, one day, would come. It was time to pack up and go over to spend some quality time with Mum—she only had a few months left. So I left my boyfriend and my job behind. Dad had also left his work a couple of months before to become Mum's full-time carer, which was literally a full-time job in its own right. I took care of everything else: my brothers; Nan (Mum's mum) who'd lived with us for 20 years; bill payments; grocery shopping; cooking meals; cleaning; washing; and driving everyone around.

'Mum went to bed one night and that was the last time I ever saw her do so. We could do nothing but watch and wait for Mum to pass away. Two straight days of no sleep and just sitting by her bedside, attached to the big teddy bear my boyfriend had bought me, watching while her body slowly shut down.

'Mum fought hard for 18 months, but she passed away in 2002 on the day after her 50th birthday and two days before Mothers Day. I was 23 years old.'

**On missing:**

'I'm now 35 years old, married and have gorgeous three year old boy/girl twins and a beautiful seven year old stepdaughter—and I struggle every day with the loss of my mum.

'I felt very lost and secretly alone for the first few months after having my twins, despite having a wonderful husband to support me. It felt then and still feels like I've lost Mum all over again. How are you supposed to do this job without your mum beside you? I'm a tough person. I have a lot of inner strength and can deal with a lot. But even now, almost 12 years later, I can't bring myself to listen to the two songs we played at Mum's funeral. I have to change radio stations or leave the room.'

# Fiona's story

## 38 years old, From Australia

**On loss:**

'At the time Mum became ill, I had three young boys and I was 31 years old. My parents lived three and a half hours away.

'It was May 2007 and Mum was diagnosed with bladder cancer. She had chemo treatment and she was told it was fine (cured). She went to the UK for a month in June to visit my little brother. She wasn't particularly well while over there and after coming home, she was made to see her doctor. Mum was the kind of woman who didn't like to worry others, especially her kids. Her motto was always, "I'm fine, I'm fine". Unfortunately, though, her visit to her doctor led to many tests and eventually a consultation with an oncologist.

'I received a phone call late one evening in early August 2007. The conversation is a blur but basically Mum said, "Fi, I have pancreatic cancer. It's terminal". I remember going downstairs to see my husband. I just cried and cried and cried. My heart felt and still does feel, like it was torn to pieces.

'On the morning of 12 January 2008, we had decided to take the kids on the train for the first time and go to the Melbourne Aquarium. I was in the kitchen making sandwiches and getting snacks organised for the trip. The phone rang with 'Mum' flashing on the screen at around 8.30am. I answered cheerily, "Good morning, how'd you sleep?". I then heard Dad on the other end, though I thought nothing strange of it. It took him a minute or two (seemed that long anyway) and then he said, "Mum's gone, Fi". I remember collapsing to the kitchen floor crying and screaming, "No, no, noooooo". My husband had to carry me to our room and he tried to shield the kids from the state I was in. I was hyperventilating, crying uncontrollably and my heart felt like it was being torn from my chest.'

**On missing:**
'I try hard to put things into perspective more. I obviously can't call Mum five times a day like I used to, so I guess I've had to learn to trust and believe in myself more now. I miss not being able to call her to tell her all about the funny, silly, stupid and lovable things the kids do on a daily basis. I'm always worried that I'm not doing things right or not doing enough and she's not here to advise me.'

**On coping:**
'I deal with Mum's loss on a daily basis. There's no rhyme or reason as to whether I'll wake up OK or depressed and missing her more than ever. If I need to cry, I do. I generally feel lighter afterwards, like I've had a big release.

'Christmas, Mother's Day, her birthday and my kids' birthdays are my biggest triggers. Without consciously thinking about it, I can feel a build-up of emotions starting about three days beforehand—this is when I will usually have a mini-meltdown, a big cry and then I'm OK. I try to keep this from the kids, but normally have to ask my husband for a hug!'

**On wishing:**
'If I could spend one last day with Mum, I'd give her the biggest, tightest hug. I'd tell her how much I love and miss her every day and thank her for being the amazing mum she was. I'd tell her how proud I am of who she was and all that she did for us. She wasn't perfect, but she did the best she knew how. I would want her to spend the day with all of her grandkids and I would just watch, take photos and cherish every single second. That would make me the happiest.'

# Julie's story
## 60 years old, From Australia

**On coping:**
'It took me five years to realise that I was beginning to deal with losing Mum. I don't remember what it was that changed. I just remember feeling more accepting about being sad, lonely and a bit lost. I remember feeling able to deal with it on my own—feeling strong enough to cope, to stand a bit taller, to learn how to take a deep breath and take a step forward. Mum would be proud of me for figuring all that out. She always knew I could be as strong as I needed to be.

'The pain isn't unbearable anymore, but for the first five or so years after she passed, I would see a lady somewhere with hair like Mum's, or who dressed the same, or who had a shopping buggy trailing along behind her. During those times, I would feel a sudden deep, heavy pain in my chest. When this happened, I would just allow myself to disappear into the crowd for a moment and become invisible until the lump in my throat settled.'

**On gains:**
'I don't take years or time for granted anymore and try to do as much as possible. I don't just wish and hope for things or experiences anymore. Instead I do all I can to 'make it happen', even if just on Mum's behalf. So now I explore hobbies, not just for me. I travel, not just for me. I surround myself with as much beauty as I can, not just for me. Wouldn't it be nice if she knew...'

**On wishing:**

'If I could spend one more day with my mum, I would introduce her to my camera, my mobile phone, my computer and Google! Mum would have loved the Internet. If she were still with us, she would be texting up a storm.

'I would also show Mum what her granddaughter is doing with the cake decorating that she so lovingly inspired. I would talk with her privately and do and say things that I could never do previously because, on my weekend visits, we were always surrounded by children and family. I would look her in the eye and tell her, "I love you".'

# Mel's story

### 35 years old, From Australia

**On loss:**

'People have asked me many times over the years if I remember my mother. I used to think that maybe I did, that if I thought hard enough a lovely memory would pop into my head. Sometimes, when I was young, I'd invent a memory to share. The truth is I don't have any memories of my mum at all. I was three years old when she died of cancer at the age of 31.

'As a kid, it was hard to grow up without a mum. I think many of my memories of it all were of being quite embarrassed at being the odd one out. It was quite well understood that some children didn't have dads around, but no one really knew what to do with me when it was time to make Mother's Day cards at school or when it was expected that mums would come up to do canteen duty. I just tried to fade into the background so there wouldn't be a scene when I was asked what day my mum could help out on sports day. Sometimes I even just said she was too busy.

'Equally bad was when a teacher knew and suddenly I was urgently needed to run an errand for her while she told the class that my mum was dead and not to say anything. It was then whispered about all day.'

**On missing:**

'When I became a mother is when I truly missed having a mum the most. I was downright jealous at times. Jealous of not having a mum to be excited at the prospect of being a grandma, to fuss over my baby, to give me advice, to love my baby. It raised questions I hadn't considered before: Was I born overdue or early?; What time was I born?; Was I a C-section?; Was I breastfed? My dad didn't know these details. Perhaps selfishly I also missed not having someone to help me out with babysitting, meals and generally just being there.

'Being without my mum has affected my parenting. I sometimes have to remind myself to kiss and cuddle my children. As much as I love them, cuddling and kissing them just isn't something I naturally do as it wasn't done to me very often.

'I feel panicked at the thought of dying on them and leaving them, particularly the girls. I feel like I sometimes have no idea what I'm doing as I've never had a proper mum.

'It has had its positives though. I remember as a child being so awestruck at going to a friend's house and her mum had baked muffins as an after-school snack. I really enjoy being able to do things like that for my children.'

# Kate's story

## 37 years old, From Australia

**On loss:**

'I was going into labour with my third son when I received the most shocking phone call from my dad. He told me that Mum was in ICU in an induced coma and things were not looking good. This was one of the most difficult times in my life. As I gave birth to my beautiful much-anticipated baby and witnessed new life unfold, my mind was also elsewhere as I prepared to say goodbye to my best friend—my beautiful mother. Miraculously, Mum overcame this present obstacle but little did I know what else my beautiful mum would have to endure.

'Mum was to face more difficult times ahead, with kidney failure resulting in the need for dialysis and hours of travel to and from treatment every second day. She was also diagnosed with multiple myeloma, or cancer of the blood. With these devastating diagnoses placing huge obstacles in her way, the treatment that would follow and the complications along the way, I saw Mum face her fears with her incredible internal strength, integrity and grace. Her days were approached with such diplomacy as she underwent her daily struggle to survive while still trying to enjoy the little things.

'I am so blessed that my mum was here for the birth of my fourth child, a daughter. The bond that I shared with Mum, the unconditional love and the friendship that we shared is so amazingly sacred and is my motivation for my life today. This strong bond, which I can see even more clearly in her absence, is my catalyst as I develop my relationship with my own daughter and sons. In doing so, I carry forward Mum's strength and honesty in raising my children and living my best life.'

## On coping:

'I miss my mum so incredibly, but what I know is that she lives in me. This woman who birthed me, nurtured me and loved me always resides in me. Our relationship continues, even in her passing, as I talk of her; share stories with my children; enjoy a sunset; look at her star; smell a flower; and enjoy a glass of wine and a private chat with her. This woman, who is so significant to me, continues to be such a strong inspiration to my days.'

## On missing:

'One of the things I miss the most is the feeling of being known. Mum knew my heart. She knew my intention. She is one person with who I could be completely myself and be raw with. She always wanted the best for me, she knew my struggles, she knew my strengths and I felt so loved. The realisation that I am now a motherless mother breaks my heart and feels so lonely, but I also know how blessed I am to have had the privilege of such a profound relationship. I will never be alone with this incredible woman in my heart. She was and still remains, my absolute best friend.'

# Emma's story

## 43 years old, From Australia

Content as appeared in 'The Canberra Times' on 12 May 2013.

**On loss:**
'You get used to not having a mum but some days, it catches you off-guard. I still go to dial the first few digits of her number or file a mental note to tell her something, usually inane, often a recipe. Then I stop and my heart begins to pound. In a shocking instant, I have to reprocess the loss all over again. She is gone and it leaves me gasping for breath. Five years on and the tears still flow with unpredictable intensity.

'I ache for her conversation. I could speak to my mum like no one else in the world. She was interested in every minute detail of my life. We would talk for hours at a stretch and then call each other on the phone to discuss the bits we'd missed. We were each other's 'other half'. It was always this way.'

**On gains:**
'I carry the weight of Mum's love with me. Her wisdom rings in my head as I go about my business of raising two children; working; cooking; cleaning; loving; laughing; and using up my own supply of days on this earth. Because Mum's death has shown me so clearly, so jarringly, that life is over very quickly. Perhaps it is the only positive thing that can be said of cancer, it leaves the ones behind with a greater

sense of what it is to live—and it gave us seven years to say goodbye in the most tender, meaningful way. We knew how much we adored each other. We knew that one day we were going to have to part. We made every year, then every month, then every day count.'

# Katie's story

## 35 years old, From Australia

**On loss:**
'I was so excited when the phone rang two days after my first daughter was born. I thought it would be my mum getting up early to call me from the UK to see how our first night at home had gone. Instead, this was a call I never in a million years thought I would receive. My husband answered and it was just horrific. It turned out that Mum had had a massive brain hemorrhage and died just 12 hours after I'd been speaking to her on Skype and showing her my daughter for the first time. No warning, no time, just the end of what I knew and the start of a very hard few years.'

**On wishing:**
'If I could have my mum back for the day—God, it's really hard to let yourself imagine something like that—I'd cocoon ourselves away, just me, Mum and the girls and spend the whole day talking, laughing and letting her get to know her beautiful grandchildren, who know exactly who she is at just three and two years of age. I would just watch them with her, cuddling her, playing with her and telling 'Nanny stories' like they tell their grandma. I'd hear my mum laughing and being silly with my girls like she did with her other grandchildren. We'd gossip like we used to and I'd get all the thoughts off my chest that, without her, now just weigh me down like an anchor.'

# Nicole's story

## 30 years old, From Australia

**On loss:**
'Celebrating the birth of my fourth child was suppose to be one of those exciting and incredibly magical times, right? Well for me, it's always going to be the start of the nearly two-year journey from when we learned of Mum's diagnosis to the day she passed.

'Following the birth of my son, Mum came to see us in hospital and just made quick mention that she was going to the doctor the next day. The following day, I received a phone call from Mum telling me that the doctor was a little concerned about fluid that was on her lung. She was being sent to see some specialists. The news wasn't good. It was stage four cancer—TERMINAL. There was an end date and it wasn't that far away. You know what though, we were blessed. We were able to spend quality time together, we could talk and just enjoy the moment.

'At approximately 7.30pm on 30 December 2011, my dad rang me to tell me that Mum had gone.'

**On missing:**
'It's been hard not having my mum around, not having a sounding board to discuss my problems, to talk to about life, to go shopping with and have girlie days. I keep my problems to myself and I think even my parenting has changed in the past two years.

'There're plenty of emotional days where you want to curl up in a ball and not leave your bed. The one thing that I'm glad we did was have family photos taken. There are photos of Mum and I that I'll cherish forever. I miss so much about her: our morning coffees when she was home from work; sitting and doing craft together; her teaching me how to sew. They are just those little moments that we'll never get back.'

# Katrina's story

## 32 years old, From Australia

**On loss:**
'One night at 2.00am, I got a phone call from my step-dad telling me that Mum had had a cardiac arrest and was in hospital. She was only 52 years old and the healthiest she'd ever been. I didn't leave my mother's side, I just couldn't. We had to make a decision to either keep her on life support or turn it off. She was brain dead and would most likely never come out of it and live a normal life again.

'On the Sunday night, we had her machines turned off to let her go. It was the hardest decision of my life and I hated having to make it. We were lucky to keep her for five more days. As she just lay there, we painted her toenails and fingernails, put her favourite perfume on and applied some makeup to make her feel better.

'On the morning Mum passed away, I was in the room with her having stayed the night. I woke up at 5.00am to her very heavy, laboured breathing. Knowing she was still there I fell back to sleep, only to be woken by the cleaner. It was then I realised that Mum was gone.

'This all happened three months before my wedding.'

**On missing:**
'On Mum's birthday, Mother's day and the date of her passing, I go to her grave with the kids and say hello—always leaving something small. Some days, I really can't cope without her here. Those are the days that

I just let myself cry. I cuddle my kids and think of all the good times we had.

'I try so hard to be beautiful, kind, caring and loving as she was, but I wish I could have her back. My daughter looks so much like my mother and every time I look at her, I see my mum smiling back.'

# Sarah's story

## 34 years old, From UK

**On loss:**

'I lost my mum in August 2007. She was 47 years old. I was aged 27 with two small children, a home and a full time job. I am also an only child.

'A routine check had revealed that Mum had a rare form of leukemia. She had ups and downs. Some days she was stronger than others. The few days after a blood transfusion were her best. I looked forward to the good days and took the hint when she wasn't up for visits.

'Things were great for a few weeks until the lead-up to Mother's Day. Mum had been suffering with sickness. Eventually, she had to be admitted to hospital as she was so poorly. I saw her as much as I could, but the logistics of visiting the hospital with a newborn and a toddler were often impossible. It was so difficult to fit in seeing her along with looking after the kids, seeing my husband and working.

'One day, the hospital rang. "Can you come up? It's your mother—she's not responding?", said the voice on the other end of the line. I had absolutely no idea what that meant or what to expect. I got to the hospital as soon as I could and was told that she'd had a huge bleed on the brain and that there was no hope. I was so confused. I was being asked to inform family, make decisions—do everything. I didn't know what to do.

'The next four weeks were just a blur. Mum never woke up. She never recovered. She slowly slipped away. I visited her; cleaned her mouth; cut her nails; put cream on her dry skin; spoke to her and told her everything. I started to realise that she would never wake up. My beautiful mum had finally given up. Her body had been battered and bruised for two long years. She was tired and enough was enough.

'The hospital called me in the early hours of 20 August 2007 to tell me to come in. I didn't make it on time. Mum had passed before I got there. I gave her a final kiss, stroked her face and left.'

## On missing:

'The things I miss the most are being able to share the milestones with Mum, share our successes—the children, our happiness. I sit and wonder whether she'd be proud of me, how she'd laugh at the children. When I send pictures of the kids to other members of the family, I long to be able to send them to her—to see her smile as she saw what she helped to create. I feel so cheated that she has been unable to see her grandchildren. I know she would have been the coolest 'Nanny' on the block.'

## On wishing:

'If I could spend one day with Mum, I would surround her with her grandchildren. I'd want her to see a glimpse of their beauty, their personalities and their intelligence. If she spent just one day with them all, she'd understand how I have the strength to carry on without her.'

# A word from the author

Dear readers,

When my mother died, I was 32 years old and I had three young boys aged eight, five and three. When it came to advice of the mothering kind, or any advice for that matter, my darling mum was the one I called on, up until she became too unwell.

It's a frightening reality when you are faced with the notion of raising children without the wisdom of someone you trust and who has walked the path. When you lose that person in your life, you have no option other than to trust your own instincts and to seek support from others whose opinions you value.

I won't lie. I am constantly stopped in my tracks as I mother my four boys. Just when I think I am excelling in my fabulous yet unrelenting daily role, a curveball is thrown and I am back to a state of utter worry and confusion (and longing for my wise mum). It's at these times that I call on my 'village of sisters'.

They say that it takes a village to raise a child and so I thought, 'Why not create a 'village of wisdom'?' Thanks to mothers from all over the world, the following pages are choc-full of support, encouragement, insight, hindsight, advice, ideas and motherly love. Here is a collection of heartfelt words that I will continually draw upon and I hope you will too. I am forever grateful to these generous mothers for sharing their wisdom and I just know in my heart that with a little bit of encouragement, your motherly walk may be a little easier and less confusing.

All my love
Leigh xxx

# MOTHER ♡

## (muhth-er) -noun

1. One person who does the work of twenty. For free.

2. Keeper of precious memories.

(see also: `saint`.)

# Words of wisdom:
## A sharing of motherly wisdom between loving mums

*'Children deserve a precious certainty that they are loved. Not because they are wonderful or clever or pretty or musical or any other attribute a child can possess, but just because they are. For no other reason than that they belong in their mother's heart forever.'*

**Joanne. My mum.**

**Forever 56.**

**Loved in the hearts of many. Always.**

# Words of wisdom:
# Life With A Newborn

Mitali
**Mother of one son aged 8 and one daughter aged 3**
**From Germany**
'Your body just created a new human being. Don't expect to feel like your former self for quite some time. For me, it took one and a half years with my son and three years with my daughter.

'Don't hate your body for not looking like it was before but appreciate it, love it, be grateful for it, for it has given you the most wonderful gift—your child!

'Be prepared to feel sleep deprived for a while, maybe for years. It is normal to wear yoga pants sometimes, to not shower in days, to not achieve anything but tending to your baby's needs. It will get better, I promise—and I had the kid who didn't sleep, at all!

'Take some time for yourself every day, even if it is just five minutes: a long hot shower; a walk around the block; a couple of minutes spent in the sunshine; enjoy a cup of coffee while reading a couple of pages of a book. This was crucial for my sanity with a baby that never slept and wanted to be breastfed every thirty minutes.'

## Kellie
## Mother of one son aged 1
## From Australia

'If your baby's asleep and you feel like having a nap, then do so. Even if it's half an hour, every little bit helps. Don't worry about the housework, seriously. In the scheme of things, the housework is not a priority.

'One thing that has stood out to me regarding my baby's sleeping is that you don't have to rush in and pick them up every time they stir or seem like they're waking up. Just pause for a minute, maybe give them a pat and you may just get an extra half hour or hour out of them.

'Please don't stress about getting back in shape the minute after you've given birth. Some people bounce back, some don't. There are far more important things going on in life than trying to jump yourself back into your skinny jeans. Don't even take them off the hanger. It took me 15 months before I was in a frame of mind to want to shed that last bit of baby weight and by last bit, I mean about 10kg. It's not a race to get back to pre-baby weight. Just do it gradually.'

## Cheryl
## Mother of one daughter aged 9 months
## From UK

'Try to go to lots of mum and baby groups for support, but try not to compare babies. Someone else's baby will always sleep though the night quicker, crawl faster, eat better and you will drive yourself nuts if you make comparisons. They are all beautifully different and get there in their own time.'

## Maria
## Mother of one daughter aged 2
## From UK

'Welcome to the new and never-before-seen chapter of your life where everything changes: your body, your hair, your relationships and your work priorities. Cry your heart out, reach out to people who resonate warmth and find comfort in knowing that there's one person in the world to who you mean the entire world right now. You're the sun, the moon and the stars to your newborn, so shine in happiness and tears.'

George
**Mother of two sons aged 9 and 6**
**From UK**
'You can never hug and hold your newborn too much. That stage doesn't last for long, so make the most of every second.

'When you feel like it is all too much, go into the bathroom, put on all the taps, flush the toilet and have a good scream/cry/sob. Then wash your face, take a deep breath and start again. You can accomplish anything if you take time to regroup.

'Be brave and trust your instincts. You can do more than you think. Ask for advice but don't be afraid to ignore it and do your own thing. Be strong in the knowledge that you are making your own way as a mother and forging your own path.

Don't compare yourself to anyone else post-pregnancy as everyone's body and metabolism is different. Be proud of your stretch marks—they are nothing to be ashamed of, they are your badge of honor!'

Lisa
**Mother of one son aged 5**
**From Australia**
'There are a lot of books out there, all made with loads of love and a world of advice. Read them, but be sure to listen to your own instincts also. Your baby needs you. It is as simple and as complex as that. Do what feels right for you and your family.'

Rachel
**Mother of one son aged 7 months**
**From Australia**
'Be kind to yourself. If you need to sleep when there are piles of laundry and chores galore waiting to be done, sleep. Try to appreciate your body, even though it looks and feels so different—it has just created a miracle! But most of all, have someone you can talk to about your thoughts. I felt like a terrible mother for some of the thoughts I was

having but, after sharing them, I realised that they were quite normal.'

## Fiona
### Mother of one daughter aged 4 and two sons aged 3 and 8 months
### From Australia

'Life with a newborn, toddlers in the mix and a debilitating, accumulating lack of sleep, all break down your resilience in ways you don't anticipate. The smallest of things become overwhelming and challenging. My mum reminded me that, "A challenge or a crisis is an invitation to dance the dance of life". So it's time to go easier on yourself: remember to nurture *yourself* with good food, sleep (when you can), stay active—and just keep on dancing.'

## Mandy
### Mother of one daughter aged 8 and two sons aged 6 and 4
### From Australia

'Everything in life functions better with sleep. Take it whenever you can and never apologise for it. I think the biggest trap for new parents is to pop their little ones down for a nap and try to nail everything else that needs to be done. Time will pass ever so quickly and all that other stuff can wait. Sleep, sleep, sleep!'

## Kathryn
### Mother of two daughters aged 11 and 7 and one son aged 1
### From Australia

'During the dark and lonely hours of feeding my baby boy, I consciously shifted my perspective and appreciated the complete peace and stillness. I reminded myself that he would only be this tiny for a couple of months. It really kept me grounded and made me grateful for that (sleepy) moment.'

## Sylvia
### Mother of one daughter aged 39 and two sons aged 37 and 33
### From Australia

'Life with a newborn is so fleeting. If I knew then what I know now,

I would have sat back and enjoyed the ride more rather than worry about doing everything right. Newborns are quite resilient. As a very young mum, I always second-guessed myself. I understand now that 'rules' are just a guide and all babies are different.'

**Livinia Nixon**
**Mother of two sons aged 4 and 1**
**Channel 9 Presenter**
**From Australia**
'When you're in the fog of exhaustion with washing, nappies, screaming babies and chaos, just remember that this is a mere moment in time. It's a fraction of a long life—until you have another baby and then it's back to the beginning for you!'

**Casey**
**Mother of one son aged 2 and one daughter aged 7 months**
**From Australia**
'Even though the nights are long, sleep is at a minimum and there doesn't seem to be light at the end of the tunnel, remember that your relationship with your partner is the reason your bundle of joy is in your arms today. You both created this little life and the love in your relationship is what will give your newborn the best start to a happy and loving future.'

**Megan Gale**
**Mother of one son aged 5 weeks**
**Model, Television Presenter and Actress**
**From Australia**
'Babies don't come with a manual and even if they did, every baby is different. They are constantly evolving and changing day to day, week to week, so it would be hard to follow instructions to the letter.

'I think it's fantastic that there is so much information out there for new mums—in books, via the internet, from friends, family members and even strangers—but it's easy to become overloaded with information. It can, at times, cloud what your natural instincts are and make you feel extremely overwhelmed. It can make you start to question what is the 'right' way to do things in regards to settling, feeding, sleeping habits (for both the baby and yourself) and so much more.

'As I write this, my little one is five weeks old and close to, what I'm told is, his peak unsettled period. What I'm finding is that it is great to store away all this information, but to not forget that we do have natural instincts as mothers. So try and go with your gut and not follow all pieces of information you receive or you'll go crazy. All the information is very polarising and what works for one person may not work for you. Store it all away, draw on what you need and have conviction on your decisions as to what you think you don't need.

'Remember, if your baby is well-fed, well-rested and well-loved then you're already doing a fantastic job.'

**Moran**
**Mother of four daughters aged 10, 8, 6 and 2**
**From Australia**
'I think that if you're not coping, just try to be honest with yourself first. We are so lucky in Australia to have excellent resources—help lines, maternal child health nurses, online forums and sleep experts. If you don't like your first port of call, find another. Keep searching till you find someone you connect with, then stick with them. I think it's better to have one trusted person/source giving you advice rather than a range.

'Babies are meant to cry, wake up and fuss. They are designed to be cuddled, held, comforted and physically close to you, especially in the first few months. Just enjoy that special time and don't worry about what other people say.'

**Leann**
**Mother of one daughter aged 15**
**From Australia**
'When people offer to help, regardless of what it is, especially in those first few weeks after you and bub come home say, "That would be most appreciated".

There is an illusion that you can be a super woman and do everything after a bub arrives. This is not the case. Choose what you can live without being done.

I used to make a list and if people offered I said, "Well I have a list. Even if one thing is marked off, that's one less for the hubby to do (lol)".

Erica
Mother of two sons aged 2 and 3 months
From Australia
'Being a mum is hard work. Feeling upset, angry, frustrated, confused, exhausted, overwhelmed—these are normal feelings and they will come and go. It can be hard to feel these things when all you're hearing from others is, "Treasure these days". Sometimes the days are hard. Remember, this too shall pass.

'Feeling totally out of your depth? Certain you have no idea what you're doing? You're not the only one, trust me. We're all pretty sure that we're doing it wrong at least some of the time. Really, you're doing a wonderful job.'

Kate
Mother of one son aged 14 months
From Australia
'Love your postnatal body. It's an amazing body—a body that has not only created life, but nurtured life and brought life into the world. Get to know and love your post-baby body because, after-all, it's a result of the beautiful little being you've brought into this world.

'Talk to your partner about how you are feeling in those early days—and keep talking to each other. Parenthood is such a huge change and strain on your relationship, especially when you don't have your own mum to lean on. Communicate about everything! Laugh, cry and stare at bub in awe together—but most of all, talk.'

**Toushka Lee**
**Mother of one son aged 6 and one daughter aged 3**
**From Australia**

'It is hard. It's harder than whatever you imagined it would be. Along with all the sleepless nights and other stuff to adjust to, will come a whole lot of advice from all corners. Take the advice with a smile and nod. Use the advice that sounds right to you. Ignore the advice that grates. Parent by instinct, not by the book or by what others will tell you is best. Believe in your instincts and follow those instincts.'

**Julia**
**Mother of one daughter aged 1**
**From Australia**

'A newborn baby is a bundle of juxtapositions that no-one can prepare you for. They will not only fill your heart with love, but also fill your eyes with tears. Their cry will make you anxious and sleepless. Your body will be weary from sleep deprivation, then absolute exhaustion, but you'll never feel more alive. You will become accustomed to feeling many highs and lows all in the same moment. In an instant, you will love and hate your partner. You will feel confident with your baby, then unsure. You will feel happiness and melancholy. You will look into your baby's eyes and feel pure love, but absolute frustration when they don't stop crying regardless of how hard you try. That tiny human will create mayhem in your life and consume all of your strength, but you will never feel more complete.

'Just remember, these highs and lows are all just fleeting moments in time. They pass. Never give up. You are stronger than you think. Even when you feel alone, in times of difficulty or despair, there will be beautiful times of joy and love only just moments away.'

**Tegan**
**Mother of one daughter aged 6 and one son aged 3**
**From Australia**

'Make time in the day to do one thing for you, be it having a shower; putting mascara on; going for a walk; or wearing your favourite earrings—anything that makes you feel normal and like yourself.'

## Sophie
### Mother of one son aged 9 weeks
### From Australia

'I'll never forget how many times I was told, "It will get better". I'd cry and think, "When?". There were nights that turned into day with no sleep. I second-guessed myself again and again, continually telling myself that I couldn't do it. I felt pain while breast-feeding and reached levels of exhaustion that I didn't know existed. Some days I'm still so busy that I don't shower and I forget to eat—but it does get better.

'Trust yourself and your mummy instincts and simply learn to accept that your baby needs you every minute of every day. My nine-week-old baby is no longer my tiny newborn and it scares me to see how ridiculously fast time flies, so enjoy it while it lasts. It does get better.'

## Jess
### Mother of one son aged 6 and one daughter aged 7 months
### From UK

'Try to remember that everything will pass. When you're so tired that you want to cry, just cry. It'll make you feel better. When they've woken up every hour for seven hours and you're dead on your feet, try to remember that no two nights are ever the same. A bad night does not mean the next will be bad too. A day and night of sickness could pass as fast as it came. They will grow! Try to enjoy the now as it goes so fast.

'It's ok to say that you're tired, you're sad, you need a break, you don't like breastfeeding, your back hurts. It's ok to ask for help, to have time to yourself. Don't feel guilty, take it—you need it. You'll benefit from it and your kids will too. A happy mum makes a happy child.'

## Maria
### Mother of one daughter aged 8 months
### From Australia

'Being a new mum, we're sleep-deprived, unsure and scared about what to do. Speak with other mums. Don't be shy to discuss what you're going through. Chances are, so many other women have experienced similar things and can share how they handled it. Take on the advice that feels right for you.'

## Rebecca Judd
### Mother of one son aged 3 and one daughter aged 5 months
### Media Personality and Author of 'Rebecca Judd Loves'
### From Australia

'Mothering a newborn is one of the hardest things you'll ever do. It is bewildering, terrifying, exciting and crazy all at once. It is ok if you feel like crying and it is ok if you feel like it's too hard. It is ok to ask for help. It is ok if you're not coping.

'Seeking guidance is not a sign of defeat. They say it takes a village to raise a child, so why do we pressure ourselves to do it on our own and feel guilty when we need help? Talk to your family, talk to your friends, talk to your mother's group—hell, chat to any mother with a child down at the park. It all helps. A few pearls I have learnt from my two babies are that:

- Breast-feeding can be easy and breast-feeding can be difficult and excruciating. Both of these experiences are normal.
- You are not a bad mother if you can't breast-feed. Formula is great!
- Newborns' tummies are a pain in the butt. Why aren't they ready for the world when they are born?
- It's ok if you stay in your PJ's all day and haven't done the washing for weeks.
- It's ok to serve your family fish fingers and freezer chips for dinner.
- Food, love and warmth are all that your baby needs to thrive. Don't stress yourself out about the details.'

Claire
Mother of two sons aged 2 and 6 months
From Indonesia

'Days four and five post-partum will feel like your entire world is about to collapse. I like to call these 'doom days'. Normally this coincides with your milk coming in and you inexplicably cry and cry (this actually really helps your milk flow. Tears flow, milk flows). Eat some chocolate, call a friend over and try to remember that this is a completely normal, hormonal reaction to birth.

'I was unprepared for how much breast-feeding sucks (literally) for the first two weeks. Prepare yourself. Get your battle head on. It is so challenging that you think you'll throw the towel in at every painful feed and then suddenly, it all clicks into place. I had an 'easy' time with my first and then my second had major latch issues! Go figure. I never take it for granted anymore. Breast-feeding takes time and patience. Block out your schedule!

'Body issues? Yikes. Lets have some perspective. You just *made an actual baby*. So things jiggle these days? So what? Jiggly bits are perfectly designed for babies to rest against.

'I was convinced, after two natural (long) births, that my entire vagina was going to fall out. Don't worry—it doesn't. Things may feel a bit, *erm*, less than optimal down there for a while, maybe months. But if your lady bits are still feeling fragile, no heavy lifting for a while, a couple of hours of horizontal legs and proper posture should improve things significantly.

'It is easy to fall into the doom. Especially when you have a newborn and a toddler tearing up the place. It's consuming and can make you lose perspective. I stuck post-it notes around the house (especially in the toilet) to refocus myself. I told myself how awesome I was, how strong I was and what an amazing job I was doing. I reminded myself that I had just given birth. 'Be gentle on myself', 'This passes', 'I have the power to heal myself', 'BREATHE'—I wrote it all down.'

**Lauren**
**Mother of one son aged 3 and one daughter aged 1**
**From Australia**

'Being a new parent is the most wonderful time. You are so taken and consumed by this new little person who has just arrived into your life. You have so much love and joy, you do really spend the first few weeks floating on a cloud. Then reality sets in a little.

'I have a newborn baby girl and my son just turned two! Going from one to two children was a huge adjustment for me initially. I had to learn to stop putting so much pressure on myself, to give in to that washing pile and list of errands. They will still be there tomorrow. Doing one thing at a time, resting when possible and just enjoying every precious moment is what really matters.'

**Amanda Holden**
**Mother of two daughters aged 8 and 2**
**Actress, Presenter and Judge on 'Britain's Got Talent'**
**From UK**

'Apart from the obvious, which is never underestimate how much having children will change you (for the better), your heart will feel open and full. Suddenly, every charitable cause, homeless person and tragedy in the world becomes all too poignant and relevant. You are suddenly aware of the world you bring your baby into. It feels all-consuming. So my advice is to never feel guilty about wishing for 7.00pm 'baby bedtime' to come along and having that glass of wine!'

**Steph**
**Mother of one son aged 3 and one daughter aged 3 weeks**
**From UK**

'Before having children, I was blissfully ignorant about how tiring and demanding the first three months with a newborn can be. With my firstborn, I really didn't anticipate how the lack of sleep and the energy demanded for breast-feeding would affect me. I was so tired all the time that I became very emotional and irrational. I probably wasn't much fun to be around for my poor husband. I had a severe case of the 'baby blues', crying at the drop of a hat and often crying for no reason. On most occasions, I didn't even know why I was crying. Nothing specific triggered the tears to flow, apart from my crazy hormones raging through my body. I didn't, in a million years, imagine this would happen. I always thought I would handle motherhood with ease, but I also had never been *that* tired.

'Thankfully, as my hormones balanced back out, the fog lifted and the tears stopped. I was finally able to enjoy my little bundle.

'I'm now three weeks into life with baby number two and thankfully, the anxiety and 'baby blues' have passed me by this time. I'm savouring every moment with my little lady.

'Be prepared for the overwhelming tiredness you will inevitably feel in the early days. Nap as much as you can during the day when your little one sleeps and don't be afraid to ask for help. Finally, be kind to yourself. You're doing the most amazing job in the world.'

Kathryn
**Mother of two sons aged 11 and 6 and one daughter aged 8**
**From Australia**
'You will experience tired like you never knew tired existed. Don't panic. It's a phase that does not last forever and believe it or not, one day you will think back fondly to late night feeds and milky burps. If women couldn't survive this bit, then the world would have ceased to exist long ago. Welcome to the 'mumma-hood'.

'Enjoy these first few short months with your baby. This is not the time to launch a new business, attend late night parties or events (that your clueless childless friends unfairly expect you to attend) or work on your bikini body so you can be ready to hit the runway next month with all the Victoria's Secret models. This is the time you care for your newborn, soak up their scent, feel their soft breath on your cheek, replenish your body, rest when you can and simply enjoy it while it lasts.

'Such sweet moments are scattered throughout, well, what can I call them? Ah yes, let's just call them 'other' moments. So to keep you sane, here are my tips.

1. In the morning, have a shower and get out of your pyjamas. You will feel better straight away.
2. Get out of the house, even if it's just a walk around the block with baby.
3. Start to shape a routine, but stay flexible which is good for both mum and bub.
4. Accept help. If someone offers to bring you a meal or do a load of washing, let them.

'Through all of this you will think, "I can't believe my mum did this for me when I was a baby". One day your baby will have the same thought about you. Being a mum is pretty special.'

**Natalie Bassingthwaighte**
**Mother of one daughter aged 4 and one son aged 1**
**Entertainer**
**From Australia**
'Life with a newborn is beyond exhausting. You have no idea what to do. What I learned is that the hard times come and go. Each 'thing' won't last forever, as much as it seems like it will. Babies are getting used to you just as much as you are getting used them. You will find your rhythm.'

**Brenda**
**Mother of one son aged 8 and one daughter aged 6**
**From Australia**
'When you bring your new baby home, your older child or children will be adapting to this change. In the early days, you'll be finding your rhythm and getting connected with your new babe as well. Have a little box of high stimulus (engaging) toys close by for your other child or children to play with while you are nursing or attending to your newborn. This box can come out at feeding time only, as a special play opportunity for your older child or children. Pack it away once you are done so they don't have too much time with it and they understand it is only for certain times of the day.'

Harriet
Mother of one son aged 5 and one daughter aged 3
From UK

'Treat being a new parent like starting a new job. Will you feel comfortable with all the new procedures straight away? Probably not, but give it a few months. Will you know all the answers and have all the solutions? Probably not, but by going with gut feelings and maybe consulting the odd manual, you will have things to try and see what works for you and your family.

'One thing to remember when going by the book is that the baby hasn't read it! Give yourself time to adjust without beating yourself up and soon you will be employee of the month—well, until the teething starts.'

Esther
Mother of one daughter aged 3
From UK

'What seems to be the biggest issue when your little one is small, no-one ever worries about once they are older. By the time your child is toddling, no-one asks how they were fed. By the time they go to school, no-one asks how old they were when they first walked. When they're teenagers, no-one asks what they were like 10 years ago. If you make choices with this in mind and choose what's best at that moment, you stop worrying as much.'

# Words of wisdom:
# Raising young boys aged 1 to 5

**George**
**Mother of two sons aged 9 and 6**
**From UK**
'They need to know is boss, so have a plan and stick to it. Have a good bed-time routine, the same every night and they will learn what comes next. This will make bedtime less stressful all-round.

'Tell them that you love them every day and they will not be afraid to show their love when they are older.

'You are their mother, not their friend. Do not get those two confused. They will have loads of friends but one only mother. They need to know that they can depend on you, that they can always come to you with anything and that you will love them no matter what.'

**Lisa**
**Mother of one son aged 5**
**From Australia**
'Boys are bursting with love for their mummies! It may not seem that way at times, though, when they challenge our every move and exert their passionate little personalities. Lead by example. They will become who you are, so be what you want them to be. Teach them from the beginning how to treat women, how to be kind, giving and gentle.'

Raychelle
Mother of two sons aged 15 and 2
From Australia
'Toddlers need lots of playtime. Real outside, dirty, bug-watching, grass-pulling, exploratory playtime. They are not made to sit still and be spectators of life. It helps them to know the earth that they live on.'

Belinda
Mother of two sons aged 4 and 2
Australia
'They need to know who is boss and who is in charge, because one day you will wake up and they will have you wrapped around their little fingers. You will be thinking, "How did it get to this?".

'Always show them love and affection and always tell them every day without fail that you love them, because boys and their mums will always have a special bond for eternity.'

Mandy
Mother of two sons aged 6 and 4 and one daughter aged 8
From Australia
'Young children have yet to learn the phrase, "Patience is a virtue" and all that it means. I've learned that children do not want to be told what they cannot do and what they cannot have. Rather, the key to avoiding a tantrum from the 'cannots' is to distract them with the 'cans'. For example, "Sorry, you can't play with that anymore because it's bath time, but perhaps you can go and pick a book out first for me to read after you've had your bath".

Terri
Mother of one daughter aged 13 and one son aged 6
From Australia
'Boys can have very quick, short tempers at this age. Teach them 'the turtle' to help them calm themselves down and to be resilient. This technique teaches them to control their tempers and avoid explosions. 'The turtle' is simply placing their arms across their chest in an X

position and tucking their head in as though they are a turtle tucking into its shell. Have them sit calmly for a minute like this.'

### Clare
### Mother of one son aged 4 and one daughter aged 2
### From Australia

'Boys need a safe space to show their emotions—to cry, be angry, get upset or whatever. Stand up for your boys when someone tries to mock or belittle that emotion.'

### Amanda
### Mother of three sons aged 13, 11 and 6
### From Australia

'As a mum to three boys (the first having now made it to his early teens) and having had the pleasure and experience of growing up with brothers, I can say that boys can appear to be weird creatures.

'Boys need rough and tumble. They need to expend energy physically and they are rarely, if ever, still. They are loud, they are risk-takers and they are insanely crazy at times.

'In these younger years, boys' development and understanding of danger and fear is delayed. They need to explore, to try things and to learn from their mistakes. Let them, but let them to do it safely. They need to run, to climb trees and chairs and tables, to roll around in the mud and to wrestle.

'Boys are curious and exploratory. They need to know how things work and often aren't satisfied with simple explanations. They will flip cars and prams over to inspect the wheel mechanisms. They will pull things apart or intensely watch how things work.

'Allow them to be boys.'

### Fiona
### Mother of two daughters aged 8 and 4 and one son aged 5
### From Australia

'Keep up the sports! Given the chance, my son would 'game' on the computer all day if he could.

Thankfully he loves football and basketball, so we encourage and support him as much as possible to keep up the physical activity. It's a great outlet. He has made new friends and is exerting all his boundless energy instead of sitting in front of the TV or iPad.'

## Michelle
### Mother of two sons aged 12 and 10
### From Australia

'I believe that surrounding yourself with friends and family who have little boys is so important at this age. Boys are busy, crazy, loud, needy and full of confidence so, within reason, you don't want to squash that at this crucial age.

'Mums need to know that their little boys are not out of control when they are, in fact, behaving normal for this age. Give them lots of love and teach them right from wrong, but be kind to yourself.'

## Erica
### Mother of two sons aged 2 and 3 months
### From Australia

'One of my favourite things to do is to spend time with other mums and their children. It gives my toddler a chance to play with his friends and me a chance to talk to some adults. If you can, surround yourself with other mums and be honest with them. Tell them about your struggles and your wins. Chances are, they can relate and it always feels better knowing you're not alone.'

## Claire
### Mother of two sons aged 2 and 6 months
### From Indonesia

'My mum told me that when disciplining a demanding toddler, to just acknowledge what he wants. For example, "Do you want the toothpaste? Yes, I *know* you want to play with the toothpaste but the toothpaste is for your teeth, not for the furniture. I *know* it is fun and you want to play with it, but it is for your teeth". Keep reaffirming, "Yes, I know what you need but this is why you can't have it". I have found that, when you do this, they are less likely to completely lose the plot. Also, it's a nice change from just having to say "No" all the time!'

## Lauren
### Mother of one son aged 3 and one daughter aged 1
### From Australia

'As a parent, we are always learning. When my boy turned three, the tantrums began. I sometimes had to ask myself, "Who is this boy and what has he done with my son?". Learning ways to handle and guide him through has made the difference. I've learned to be organised, set boundaries, give lots of encouragement when he's trying new things and have rewards ready when needed. I believe these things will help my son to hopefully grow up to be a courteous, confident and loving young man.'

## Emily
### Mother of two sons aged 5 and 2
### From Australia

'My boys are aged five and two. They are sponges for all things magical, fantastical and impossible. They are small, but have enormously inquisitive minds and possess an amazing ability to see things as abstract. People can have three heads and five legs, dragons can live under their beds, a tree stump is a rocket and a stick is a wand. Don't squash this imagination—let it grow. Let their world be illustrated in luminous technicolour. I have seen through my mother's death that adults' worlds are too black and white: too much life and death, too much yes or no, not enough perhaps or maybe.

'I want to hold these little boys' hands so tight so they don't fall, so they don't have to see any dark places and they don't need to be scared. Yet if I don't let them fall, they won't learn to get back up and try again and again. Children need the belief that they are strong enough to stand for themselves as themselves. As my mum baked bread and cakes with my eldest son, I can hear her saying, "Let the boys be pink, purple or blue. Let them nurse a doll, be a princess, believe in fairies, paint their faces with butterflies or monsters. Let them wear your shoes. Let them dance, let them sing. Let their dolls and dinosaurs drive fire engines. Let them cuddle, kiss and cry. Let them know that they are beautiful. Let them fundamentally know that their feelings are their own and nobody else's".

'It is only by me letting these little boys own their world that they will believe they have the strength to take it on—to take on the stars and soar beyond their dreams as their grandma always knew they could.'

## Kayleigh
**Mother of one son aged 2**
**From UK**
'Embrace their individuality. It's so easy to be drawn into comparisons, especially with children of a similar age. Show them love and encouragement and embrace their quirks. I've found that trying to make them do what everyone else's child is doing will only make you both stressed and upset if it's not what they want or can achieve. They'll all meet their learning targets in time anyway.'

## Chloe
**Mother of two daughters aged 8 and 7 and three sons aged 5, 4 and 10 months**
**From UK**
'Choose your battles. Does it really matter if he has the purple spoon over the one you've selected? No. Does it really matter if he says "Please" and "Thank you"? Yes. You could spend your entire day going head-to-head, but really? It's exhausting. So be sure of what is worth fighting for but once you decide, stick to your guns. Providing clear, definite boundaries is so incredibly important. Be firm and be fair.'

## Brenda
**Mother of two sons aged 8 and 6**
**From Australia**
'At the ages that your child begins to attend pre-school and school, it is a great time to get them understanding responsibility in the home.

Setting small, achievable chores or tasks for them to do at home is a great way to start. Have them watch you make their bed, and allow them to do the final stage. Perhaps they could help set the cups on the table for dinner. Packing up is always an important responsibility and perhaps setting up a reward chart with stickers or stamps for compliance will encourage them too. Then, as they get older, the responsibilities can increase and become more complex.'

**Amy**
**Mother of three sons aged 5, 3 and 9 weeks**
**From Australia**
'Give your boys firm boundaries and stick to them. Rules and structure will create an understanding of your expectations of their behaviour as they grow and they will respect and listen to you when it really counts.

'Teach them to cook with you. Nourish them with the joy of meals together. We talk about our favourite part of the day at our family dinners. Every family member takes their turn and it makes us appreciate how lucky we are.'

# Words of wisdom:
# Raising young girls aged 1 to 5

**Mitali**
**Mother of one son aged 8 and one daughter aged 3**
**From Germany**
'Read lots of books with different female characters in them: princesses, pirate girls, stay-at-home mums, working mums, fairies and witches. Your daughter needs to know that she can be anyone she wants to be!'

**Kelly**
**Mother of one son aged 5 and one daughter aged 3**
**From UK**
'Take advantage of any cuddle she gives. My daughter is independent and gives cuddles when *she* wants to. Cherish them!

'Tantrums are more long-lived. Walk away. Let her simmer. She'll come around, sometimes as long as an hour later.

'Independence: it's challenging, but let it happen. Be there when she needs you, but let her have some time to do what she wants. Apparently challenging behaviour often comprises the attributes that we want our kids to have in later life, so embrace it—even when that's hard to do.

'Clothing is important for my girl. If she wants to wear pj's to her nursery then why not? It's embarrassing, but I let her do it and take her clothes in to let them change her when she's ready. I have never picked her up in her pj's yet! Also, what does it matter if she wants to wear spots and stripes in colours that don't match? Laugh. Personalities are in the making, so don't make them feel embarrassed by what they say or do.'

### Jodeen
### Mother of two daughters aged 4 and 2
### From Australia

'These early years are such a great time of change, growth and development. While setting boundaries and showing them right from wrong, we also try to listen to them and let them work through their emotions. Most of all, we have encouraged them to have fun, learn from their mistakes, enjoy life and love with all their hearts.'

### Jane
### Mother of one daughter aged 4
### From Canada

'What have I learned during the past four years with my little one? Mostly, that we are all in this together. I don't know how I would have done remotely as well if I didn't make contact with as many other moms as I could. Advice ranging from brands of strollers, diaper creams, husband issues and what type of clothing to get has all been solicited from other moms and gratefully implemented. These are both moms that I already knew or have simply struck up conversations with while out and about. I now help out any new mom that I possibly can, always with the caveat that, "If this works for you then great, if not then you need to do what is best for your family".'

### Natalie Bassingthwaighte
### Mother of one daughter aged 4 and one son aged 1
### Entertainer
### From Australia

'My daughter is very sensitive in large social situations, often not wanting to join in. This can make you feel worried that they will never fit in. Allow your children to go at their own pace. Encourage and support their choices. They will get there.'

Terri
Mother of one daughter aged 13 and one son aged 1
From Australia

'Not all girls like dolls and tea parties. Some prefer climbing trees and wrestling. Accept them for who they are and don't push them into a stereotype. She is who she is. Love her unconditionally.'

Clare
Mother of one son aged 4 and one daughter aged 2
From Australia

'I try to emphasise good things about my daughter that aren't tied to her looks. It's hard when that's what society shouts at her, but I still try.'

Moran
Mother of four daughters aged 10, 8, 6 and 2
From Australia

'The inevitable bitchiness among girls does happen. A psychologist once told me that one of the ways in which boys and girls differ is how they play. Boys will set the rules quickly and play their game. Girls will spend their time negotiating the roles and rules of the game, more so than actually playing the game! This means that girls develop great negotiation skills. Unfortunately, they can also negotiate each other out of the game.

'Have a moral compass about what "we" do as a family, such as "We don't exclude people" and "We don't hit". Reinforce regularly how much you value this kind of behaviour.'

Tegan
Mother of one daughter aged 6 and one son aged 3
From Australia

'Being outdoors is free: walking on the beach or in the bush, playing in the sand, swinging on the swings at the park, collecting stones, making fairy houses. Whatever the weather, make the most of the outdoors with your child. Adventure and discoveries make beautiful memories.'

### Kylie
**Mother of one son aged 10 and three daughters aged 9, 5 and 4**
**From Australia**

'Encourage resilience and determination early. It's ok to not get things right the first time. You need to keep trying to be good at something. Feedback is good as we learn all the time. Even when we are adults, we make mistakes. If your little princess falls over and scrapes herself, encourage her to get back up, wash it and go back to playing.'

### Jo Stanley
**Mother of one daughter aged 5**
**Comedian, Writer, Television and Radio Presenter**
**From Australia**

'The gifts my daughter has brought me are many: to feel a purpose in life that I never thought possible, to feel surrounded by love and to feel like I'll never be alone again.

'My sole objective as her parent is to guide her through lessons about herself and the world around her and through that learning, to help her genuinely like herself. She gives me the cues to her needs. All I have to do is listen and *never* impose my own expectations on her because when I do that, I close off her teachings to me. My role is to be present, authentic and loving. In doing so, our communication is completely open and we learn together.'

### Chloe
**Mother of two daughters aged 8 and 7 and three sons aged 5, 4 and 10 months**
**From UK**

'Tell her that she's beautiful, clever, magical, wonderful, funny, strong and fierce, but don't make any single one more important than the other. She will spend her life being bombarded with the idea that her appearance matters more than her abilities, but that's tosh. Also, never let her hear you say a bad word about yourself. Own when you make mistakes, but don't let her see you thinking you're fat or ugly. Your kids think you're beautiful and amazing, so give it a go.'

# Words of wisdom:
# Raising young boys aged 6 to 12

**Mitali**
**Mother of one son aged 8 and one daughter aged 3**
**From Germany**

'Be clear in what you expect from your son, such as cleaning his room and paying attention in school. Don't be mad if he just lives in his own world and forgets half the stuff you want from him half the time, though. He doesn't do it to annoy you. He just has so many new thoughts in his head that all this "Clean your room" and "Don't forget your homework" business is too much for him sometimes.'

**Kellie**
**Mother of two sons aged 7 and 4**
**From Australia**

'As my eldest son (who is now seven) has grown, I've found him to express feelings and emotions through words a lot less. I know it's a common 'boy thing', but it was making me feel sad to lose this connection so early. So instead of pushing for information at any time during the day, I wait until my son is settled in bed. I turn out the light, kneel down to lean on his bed and start with a quietly spoken positive comment. It can be anything: "You had a big smile when you finished school", or "Today I remembered the time you did a great trick at the skate park".

'If I've been concerned about behaviour or want to know about his day, I bring this up gently and find that the response is honest, friendly and forthcoming. He actually wants to chat and reveal his insecurities or emotions, even if it's just for five minutes. I get more out of him during this peaceful time than any other and he gets my undivided attention. It's priceless for us both and is my favourite time of day.'

Terri
**Mother of one daughter aged 13 and one son aged 6**
**From Australia**
'Enjoy cuddles wherever you can. Boys are very loving and warm and will learn to mirror devotion to others when it is shown to them.'

Louise
**Mother of one daughter aged 18 and two sons aged 13 and 9**
**From Australia**
'Let boys be boys. Turn off the TV and Xbox and get them outside. Get them walking, climbing and exploring. Get them stimulated and see their imaginations flourish. They need activity and fresh air, though it will take some time from you to instigate this. What do boys want at this age? Quality family time.'

Amanda
**Mother of three sons aged 13, 11 and 6**
**From Australia**
"Bum' and 'poo' are the funniest words in the world. Penises are hilarious too and you can expect to see and hear lots of this kind of talk. It's not intended to offend or upset, it's just funny—apparently.

'Guns and swords are also a part of their play. They can turn anything into a gun or sword: sticks, Lego, even your entire cutlery drawer. They're not freaks, they're not deranged or psychologically damaged and they're not likely to grow up to be axe-murderers or serial killers.'

April
Mother of four sons aged 10, 6, 2 and 8 months and one daughter
aged 8
From UK
'When a boy is growing up, he is constantly told: "Be brave", "Boys
don't cry", "Don't be a wimp" and "You're a big boy now". But there are
times in a boy's life when he doesn't want to be brave. He wants to
cry instead. He wants to just be his age. These are the times when he
needs the arms of his mother to make him feel that he can be himself.
Boys need so many hugs and so much comfort! They are beautiful
little souls who just need love.'

Lianne
Mother of one son aged 9 and two daughters aged 16 and 5
From Australia
'Boys are tough yet uncomplicated. My nine year old basically consists
of: a need to know what the next meal is and what it includes, annoying
his sisters, sailing and playing footy with his friends at school. I love
him, but he is somewhat of a foreigner to me as I grew up without
brothers. That's why my approach includes God. I'm all about trying
to give him a sense that life is bigger than his perceptions of who he is
now, that he has been created for a life of significance and purpose—
however that looks.'

Tracey
Mother of three sons aged 10, 8 and 5
From Australia
'I believe that raising children of any gender and age is a day-by-day,
moment-by-moment journey. One of the best things I learned early on
is to accept advice (and filter it) from wise people who have been where
you are already. Such people could be anyone from an older woman
down the street or in a book to another school mum.

'One thing that I learned many years ago in relation to boys was
that to get them to do things, a challenge must be set. Most boys can't
resist a challenge. For example:

Me: "I just don't know if you're strong enough to take this bag of rubbish to the outside bin?"

Boy: "Just watch me!"

And that's another job done! Most of the time, it works a treat in getting stuff done.

'Another thing I read a long time ago was how important touch is for boys. This can take the form of cuddles or, for the less cuddly, just a pat on the back or hand on the shoulder will do. Contact sport will also help your boy get the touch he needs in an extremely masculine way. So if your boy is having a bad day, grab him and give him a squeeze, or maybe an arm wrestle will do it, but give your boy the contact he needs each day.'

## Amber
### Mother of two sons aged 10 and 8
### From Australia

'We have a saying in our house that, "There is a fun way to do almost everything". Sometimes I forget that but, when I remember, everything *shifts*. I believe in clear boundaries but I also know that, while our children are growing up and becoming more independent by the day, they're still kids. They still want to have fun and know that they are loved.

'Parenting is hard. It's confusing and stressful at times, but our kids love to see us laugh, play games, be silly and let our guard down. Fun builds relationships and trust and eases stress. So the message I want to share is: "Go and give someone a big, fat, noisy raspberry, then find the *fun* way to do what has to be done".'

# Words of wisdom:
# Raising young girls aged 6 to 12

**Angela Mollard**
**Mother of two daughters aged 13 and 10**
**Columnist, Commentator and Author**
**From Australia**

'Don't be hung up about your body. Walk around the house naked, talk about bodies and tell your daughters what you love about your body, pointing out what it does for you, how it makes you feel. For instance, when I'd come back from a swim I'd say how fantastic I felt, how healthy.

'I don't have scales so they can't see me weighing myself and I lie about in my knickers all the time. If you want your daughter to feel good about her body, you have to show her how great you feel about your own.'

**Lisa**
**Mother of one daughter aged 11**
**From Australia**

'Always be ready to listen. We're all busy, but sometimes these little people just need a sounding board. If you can contribute a positive solution to current worries, even better.'

Mandy
**Mother of one daughter aged 8 and two sons aged 6 and 4**
**From Australia**
'As my daughter grows, she no longer wants me to do things for her. Rather, she wants to do things together. She doesn't want a mother who is too busy, unless it is busy with her. There has been a shift in our activities. I no longer go to the gym as, instead, I go for a run while she rides her bike. I honestly think she just desires that one-on-one time to have stimulating conversations that show her she is loved.'

Patrycja
**Mother of two daughters aged 7 and 5 and one son aged 3**
**From Switzerland**
'I have just entered this stage and already, it has become incredible to me to see the importance and challenges that friendship brings into the lives of little girls. Our lifestyle means that we have travelled a lot and so, from a very young age, our children have had to learn to make friends and say goodbye to friends as well. What has been amazing to me is seeing how complex friendships can be among little girls. How alive competitiveness, fitting in and being 'best friends' is in the language and games they play and how rapidly the labels change from day to day.

'I am also witness to their ability to resolve things on their own without intervention, simply by being given the right tools—tools based on kindness, respect and honesty for each other and for themselves.'

Terri
**Mother of one daughter aged 13 and one son aged 6**
**From Australia**
'Girls will ask you curly questions about their body changes and other 'growing issues'. Don't lie to them. Always have an answer ready and be honest. If you are not sure how to answer certain questions, tell them that you'll get back to them when you have thought of a way to explain it in which they can understand. Better they learn the truth from you than some story on the playground.'

## Louise
**Mother of one daughter aged 18 and two sons aged 13 and 9**
**From Australia**
'Girls need friends. They need to feel part of a group. Support them in creating this social network. They will love to chat and to create. Get the girls together for a 'making day'. Make some masks, cakes, pottery and visualisation boards: doing, making and chatting.'

## Fiona
**Mother of two daughters aged 8 and 4 and one son aged 5**
**From Australia**
'Always try to keep communication lines open. If we're having a discussion about something that's affecting my eight year old daughter, such as a problem with a teacher, I let her know that she can tell me and I assure her that I won't be angry or cross. I want her to feel comfortable opening up to me about anything and everything. I even tell her that I won't look at her while she says it. We go forward from there with strategies and discussions, then cuddles and reassurance that it will all be ok.'

## Coral
**Mother of two daughters aged 13 and 9 and two sons aged 11 and 6**
**From UK**
'My oldest daughter has just turned 13 and while I look on in wonder at the little lady she is becoming, my heart hurts with all the insecurities and awkwardness that turning into a teenager brings. It is a hard transition to turn from a little girl into a woman and this process takes a long time.

'As mummies, we need to provide a safe environment for our daughters to explore who they are becoming. Choose your battles wisely, forgive easily, encourage respect and love for others but most of all, do whatever you can in your power to help your daughter respect herself and be proud of her place in the world. Our daughters should not be who we want them to be but the person they want to be. We should support and encourage that.'

### Moran
### Mother of four daughters aged 10, 8, 6 and 2
### From Australia

'I think a really important buzzword for kids now is 'resilience' in life. This means not just bouncing back from adversity but bouncing forward. We should stop wanting our kids to be happy and pulling those strings for them, but rather let them experience frustration and setbacks. This, after all, is what happens in adult life. We can't rush in and fix every problem. Let kids experience the consequences of behaviours so that they can learn.

'I think communication is so important. Start a healthy dialogue about issues that may become complicated as they get older. For example, talk about how friends should treat each other, body issues, being healthy and body safety. Your kids have to know that these are things we talk about at home comfortably. I also think this is important so that if they see inappropriate behaviour, such as someone being bullied, you've already laid foundations for them to recognise when something doesn't seem right and know they can talk to you about this.'

### Leann
### Mother of one daughter aged 15
### From Australia

'Allow them to do all of the things that we took for granted. Let them get dirty, play in the mud, have a cubby house, ride a bike, explore nature and have a dog. All of these things build imagination and when they hit their teenage years, it's this creativity that will help boost their grades. Time invested here is time well spent.'

### Tegan
### Mother of one daughter aged 6 and one son aged 3
### From Australia

'Find time in your day to just sit, talk or play with your daughter at this age. They love talking to their mum, so encouraging that connection and open communication can only help make a smoother path as they grow. You'll create beautiful memories along the way too.'

Kylie
Mother of one son aged 10 and three daughters aged 9, 5 and 4
From Australia
'Once at school and around ages seven to eight, girls try their absolute hardest to please everyone including themselves. This puts a lot of pressure on them, so much so that when they get home after a long day, they need to vent. This can take the form of screaming and temper tantrums.

'Let your daughter know that it's ok to vent, but not ok to take it out on other members of the household. Instead, come up with strategies together to help her deal with her stress. For example, we made a chart in my daughter's room which included ideas of what she could do after a stressful day or when she was feeling angry. Some of the ideas were to have a bath, draw a picture, listen to music, read a book, keep a diary and take the dog for a walk around the block. She now feels empowered to make the right choice and we have a happier household.'

Lu
Mother of two daughters aged 13 and 8
From Australia
'When my youngest daughter makes any request, such as asking me to run a bath for her or to teach her how to play solitaire, I remind myself that one day she won't ask for my help anymore. As a parent, I am helping to create memories for her to take into adulthood.'

Rachael
Mother of two daughters aged 9 and 7
From Australia
'Young girls need to know that they are loved and valued. They need to know that there is a safe, reliable person with who they can always communicate, whenever they need to.

'They need to be encouraged and championed on in their journey. Some little things that I love to do include writing post-it notes that I put in their lunch boxes to remind them how much they are loved and cherished. Both my girls also have a small white board in their room. Each night, we write a little sentence for them like: "You are a champion" or "You are so loved and adored". They also write little notes to us. This keeps the communication lines open and our written messages place worth on them from the moment they wake up and read these.

'We make story time a priority at night as this is quiet time together. It's also valuable to schedule in 'dates' with your daughter. Spend one-on-one time doing something you both enjoy, such as baking or visiting a cafe. When daughters know deep in their heart how valuable, loved and safe they are, it makes some of life's experiences—such as friendship issues and bullying—a little easier to tackle.'

### Chloe
**Mother of two daughters aged 8 and 7 and three sons aged 5, 4 and 10 months**

'Suddenly, your beautiful squishy parcel will have opinions, thoughts and friendships away from you. It is a strange and upsetting process, but it happens. Encourage them, support them and most important of all, listen to them. They may seem suddenly all grown up, but they are still fragile little things that need your love and reassurance.'

### Vicci
**Mother of one son aged 14 and one daughter aged 11**
**From UK**

'Young girls approach their teenage years far earlier than they used to. In our house, we re-named the age of 10 as 'tenteen' and age 11 as 'eleventeen'! At around these ages, girls start to define themselves and begin to let go of their parents. This is a natural process and as parents we watch and wait, remaining by their side should they need to return close by or step away. It's a slow process and can be turbulent, however, letting them make some decisions and choices of their own is a good practice. Pick the decisions and choices that you are willing to let them make based on what could happen if it goes wrong, that is, keep it low risk.

'I have always thought that openness about our bodies is the best policy. This has served me well, as I've found out about all kinds of things and have been able to step in and offer advice along the way. My daughters and I have talked about everything from head lice to wearing deodorant.'

## Rebecca
### Mother of two daughters aged 10 and 5 and one son aged 9
### From Australia

'When my 10 year old is having a meltdown and I'm at breaking point, I take a deep breath and I hug her. I tell her that I love her and I hold her, even when it's the last thing I want to do. It calms her down, it calms me down and then we can talk about the problem properly, without the anger and emotion. Sometimes when you just want to push them away, this is when they need you to hold them the most.'

## Joanna
### Mother of one daughter aged 6 and one son aged 2
### From Canada

'Find things that you can do together. Gently encourage her to try different activities, help her find her passion and support her in anything she wants to do.

'Talk about anything and everything, agree, disagree, argue, laugh, listen to her without judgement and let her speak. Watch the words, attitude and tone of voice you are using because she will speak to you in the same way.'

# Words of wisdom:
# Raising teenage boys aged 13 to 19

**Leisa**
**Mother of one son aged 16 and one daughter aged 14**
**From Australia**
'It's never wrong to show emotion. Boys can cry. Always tell your boys that you love them so it's natural for them to say it back with feeling. Then they will kiss you goodbye wherever you are and kiss you hello when they see you.'

**Raychelle**
**Mother of two sons aged 15 and 2**
**From Australia**
'Teenage boys need to be reminded multiple times a day that you love them. Their lives are so busy with school, sport and social activities that we can sometimes think they are raising themselves. Yet they need a mother's love even more so to remind them that the world is still a loving, caring place.'

**Emma**
**Mother of two sons aged 17 and 9**
**From UK**
'Your boy will turn from your beautiful little angel into a hor-mone-filled, raging adolescent. There will be times when you don't like

him. There may even be times when you feel like you hate him and he will feel exactly the same about you. This is normal, but don't turn your back on him.

'Don't let him feel alone, but be honest. Tell him that, even though you might not like him very much at the moment, you love him with all your heart and nothing can ever change that. Reassure him that your love is unconditional. Let him know that you have loved him from the moment he was the size of a pin-head, that his life is just beginning and you will love him until the end of time. He might not seem to be listening and he might grunt, shout and scream, but he needs to know that your love for him is constant—that he is your world, your everything and nothing can ever change that.

'Teenagers need you as much as toddlers do. They need you to be at home worrying about where they are. They need conformation and affirmation that they're doing OK. They need your love and support now as much as they did when they were little.'

## Sylvia
### Mother of one daughter aged 39 and two sons aged 37 and 33
### From Australia

'Teens! This is a scary time for most parents. I still remember this as the scariest time of our lives, but the rewards were also amazing.

'I had a few challenging teenagers who certainly got into some strife. I clearly remember my husband saying to my son, when he was about 13 or 14, that there was nothing he could do that would make him unwelcome to come home—ever. That was the rule: whatever they did, we would work it out. We sure had some sleepless nights, but we made it clear that we would always back our kids. My husband was kicked out of home when he was 14 for being a 'stupid kid' and he vowed that it would never be like that for his children.

'Other than having you provide a secure and loving home, your teen's peer group is the most important thing at this age. Help your kids choose their friends wisely.'

## Louise
**Mother of one daughter aged 18 and two sons aged 13 and 9**
**From Australia**

'So the hibernation begins. I have seen it many times now with my stepsons. Allow them to sleep, to hibernate, though give them a responsibility too. Take them out and turn technology off one day a week. Kiss and hug them, though not in front of their mates. They secretly love it.'

## Amanda
**Mother of three sons aged 13, 11 and 6**
**From Australia**

'Girls may still "have germs" or they may start taking a mild, physical attraction to members of the opposite sex. They are still very capable of having girls as friends, even best friends, without you needing to worry about anything.

'They are starting to do more without you and rely on you less for input into their lives. They will find their own way to friends' houses, start organising things on their own and become more independent. This is partly due to the fact that you are now "so old" and "don't understand kids these days". You suddenly shift from 'knower of all' to 'knower of nothing', but they will still come to you when they need a hug, if they're feeling sad or just need you to make their lunch for school.'

## Marguerite
**Mother of twin sons aged 21 and one daughter aged 19**
**From Australia**

'Ensure they have learned good hygiene practices and become friends with deodorant, because boys in this age range can stink!

'Help them to look after their skin because pimples and acne really affect their self-confidence and self esteem.

'Never make mention to them of any 'wet' sheets or pj's that require washing. Accept that this is a normal part of male adolescence and do not make a fuss.'

Helen
Mother of one daughter aged 17 and one son aged 13
From New Zealand

'I believe that boys need to be given the message to expose a range of emotions, not just anger. My son often tries to hide it when he is upset about something. I encourage him to talk about why he feels the way he does. Too many older men think that they're not being strong if they show their caring, more vulnerable side. Doing so is a skill that has to be taught.

'I also believe it's very important for boys to have friends of both sexes, particularly if they don't have female siblings. Encourage them to be friends with boys so that they can be their 'boysie' selves and also with girls, so that they will be encouraged to develop their other life skills like listening and compassion. Boys who have strong female friendships when they are younger, will grow up to be far better male companions.'

Emma
Mother of two sons aged 13 and 2 and one daughter aged 12
From Australia

'When it hits you one day like a tonne of bricks that your boy is growing up, be kind to yourself. He will no longer feel like a child, but all you will see is your baby. Take time to allow yourself to feel, get out the baby photos and treasures you have held onto and cry. Then look at your young man with pride, for both who he has become and who he will be.'

Vicci
Mother of one son aged 14 and one daughter aged 11
From UK

'It's important to remember that our children are individuals. Each child is unique. Comparing your child to others and against academic 'expectations' isn't necessarily helpful. I firmly believe in raising a teenage boy who is a well-rounded individual and happy with who he is. I will be proud of him whatever he does in life.

'Balance and perspective are important, otherwise we can become consumed with other people's standards and expectations. If people were all meant to be the same, we would be. Enjoy your son for who he is and be proud.

'Boys can be sulky and head-strong. I think it is definitely worth picking your battles and letting them win some. Lead by example and if your son proves you wrong, apologise. They will appreciate your honesty and will readily apologise to others when they are wrong.'

## Kathryn
## Mother of two sons aged 11 and 6 and one daughter aged 8
## From Australia

'Here's a tip from a friend, who got it from a friend, about how to deal with the sticky/crunchy sheet situation that is common among teenage boys—awkward. She said that the kindest thing you can do for your son is to make it a family routine that every Saturday (or whenever), everyone takes their own sheets off their own beds and puts them into the washing machine. You teach him how to turn the machine on, dry his sheets and put them back on his bed. Aside from doing his future partner a service, you are giving him skills so that on a Wednesday morning, if his sheets need 'refreshing', he knows how. That way, changing his own sheets will not be unusual for him and most importantly, he doesn't have to die of embarrassment asking you to do it.'

# Words of wisdom:
# Raising teenage girls aged 13 to 19

**Melissa**
**Mother of two daughters aged 15 and 13 and one son aged 10**
**From Australia**
'Communication with teenage girls is hard, especially when they hate you and are mad, embarrassed, humiliated, devastated or just confused. The thing that works for me and mine, in all situations at any time of the day, is texting. They text me whenever they want to about whatever they feel. It's raw, honest and works without judgement or problems.. Communication is the key, so do this any way you can. This is how your teenage girls know they can talk to you about what is going on for them. It really works.

**Alicia**
**Mother of two daughters aged 18 and 12**
**From Australia**
'As a mother of two girls, I often worried that they wouldn't talk to me about the things closest to their hearts. This was the case between my mother and me. I read somewhere that to encourage your kids to open up to you, you don't ask them what's going on. Instead, you simply *do* something with them on their own, like a walk, cooking or shopping. This was so true for my girls. I could not believe the things that were revealed to me on a casual walk around the block or along the river. It

opened a gateway of real communication between us that continues today.'

## Elva
**Mother of two sons aged 57 and 51 and one daughter aged 54**
**Australia**

'When my daughter was aged 16 to 17, she was a loving daughter one day but the opposite the next. When she was refused permission to go away with a group I did not trust, she left home and I was devastated.

'Eight months later, my daughter was told we were going on a family holiday for a couple of weeks. Our girl asked if she could come with us. We, of course, said yes. Our daughter was safely back under our roof. Thankfully, our door was never closed to her. We did not talk much about that time in our lives as forgiveness is a two-way street. Now, 36 years later, we still have a great relationship.'

## Daniela
**Mother of two daughters aged 16 and 14**
**From Australia**

'The best thing I have done as a parent is to be very open and discuss everything with my girls. If they have a question, I always do my best to answer it openly and honestly in an age-appropriate manner. I now find that as teenagers, they are open and honest in return.'

## Sylvia
**Mother of one daughter aged 39 and two sons aged 37 and 33**
**From Australia**

'Bullying is so rife at this age. If I had my time again, I would handle this issue differently. One of my children was bullied at school, but I didn't realise the lasting effect this has. Don't ignore bullying. Tackle the school, jump up and down and make it a big issue. Kids cannot sort this out for themselves. It is too difficult. We have to be our children's biggest advocate, especially when they are teenagers.

'Don't sweat the small stuff. If it's not important, ignore it but kids need boundaries. If you don't agree with something, don't allow it. It's fine to be the 'mean mum'. It shows kids that you are prepared to make the unpopular choices, which are always the harder choices, because you love them.'

## Marguerite
### Mother of twin sons aged 21 and one daughter aged 19
### From Australia

'Teenage girls are always testing the boundaries. They will try to make you feel bad or guilty by saying things like, "But Jane's parents let her". Don't fall for it. Have clear boundaries and rules in place and stick to them.

'Once puberty hits, mood swings are the norm. There will be slammed doors, rolled eyes and maybe even some, "I hate you's". Understand that this is normal and don't let it upset you.'

## Lisa
### Mother of two daughters aged 18 and 16
### From Australia

'Be a positive role model for your daughter as she makes her way through the challenging teenage years. Don't just pay her lip service. Honour the love you have for her and be honest. Be honest with yourself too. If you are encouraging your daughter to act a certain way, some self-reflection can be helpful.

'Tell your daughter that she is smart, funny, kind, beautiful and resilient. Tell her she is strong and even though bad things may happen, she will always be loved and she will get through it.

'Let her know that her body is for dancing, running, working and playing, so she needs to fuel and nurture it.

'Encourage her to laugh often, wear her smile with pride and be friendly. Let her make her own mistakes and be there with a cup of tea and a tissue when she needs it.

'Remember that, no matter what life throws at you, you are an amazing woman and mother. One day you will see a confident young woman walking down the road. You will notice how beautiful she is and how happy she looks, then you will realise that she is your little girl and your heart will be full.'

Helen
Mother of one daughter aged 17 and one son aged 13
From New Zealand

'I always tell my daughter that the key to successful friendships, first and foremost, lies in trust and honesty. Laced with a little humour and kindness, we have formed a relationship based on these principles and we have one of the best mother/daughter relationships that I know. I have conversations with my daughter that my mother would never have had with me, perhaps for fear of embarrassment or just the consideration that they were 'no go' areas.'

Leann
Mother of one daughter aged 15
Australia

'Teenagers need more hugs and understanding than they did when they were six years old. Uncertainty and confusion comes about as their frontal cortex undergoes redevelopment. This redevelopment last for about seven years and is responsible for making your child selfish and conceited. Learning to listen without offering unsolicited advice is the most beneficial quality a parent can have.'

Beccy
Mother of one daughter aged 21 and three sons aged 4, 2 and 10 months
From Australia

'Just remember that, overnight, you will go from being cool to being the most embarrassing person on the planet. They become extremely emotional little beings. Be there for them and listen, but keep a tight reign on them. You are not their best friend, you are their mum. They need hugs and kisses when they still want to be a child. Then, when they feel that they are growing up, they need rules and for you to be emotionally present.

'If you don't know how to use social media, start learning!

'Be strong. For me, the teenage years were the hardest but most rewarding times.'

Lu
**Mother of two daughters aged 13 and 8**
**From Australia**
'With so many changes happening for girls in early teen-hood, I like to talk with my daughter while brushing her hair or giving her a back rub. I chat about what she may experience and how it's normal to feel emotional, overwhelmed—even angry.

'At times, she needs as much nurturing as a toddler. Sometimes she just wants me to listen and sometimes she just needs be alone. Reading and respecting her cues is the key.'

Nathalie
**Mother of one daughter aged 18 and one son aged 9**
**From Australia**
'Imagine that you have a time machine and set the destination back into the past to your teenage years. Remember and re-live the intense emotions you experienced. The highs, the lows and the 'no-one understands' me phase. The transition into adulthood brings a whole new realisation of life. No longer is everything easy or fun. The innocence of childhood seemingly disappears overnight.

'Make time for your teenage daughter. Arrange to walk together, have cuddles on the couch or cook together. Keep connecting, listen to what she says, laugh and cry together. Be there, she needs you more than she thinks she does.'

Jo
**Mother of two sons aged 23 and 21 and one daughter aged 16**
**From United Arab Emirates**
'After raising two teenage boys, a teenage girl was quite a shock. The tightly wound coil of a teenage girl's hormonal-driven existence can be quite a challenge. One minute all is well then the next, there's a fog of unreasonable and inexplicable angst that then clears without rhyme or reason.

'Decisions are governed by peer pressure, plans change continuously and parents are seen as the absolute embarrassment—and we aren't even that bad! It's a rocky and unpredictable journey, but it's fun too as you watch the teenager wrestle the child from within and grow towards adulthood.'

# Words of wisdom:
# Adulthood and beyond

**Sylvia**
**Mother of one daughter aged 39 and two sons aged 31 and 33**
**From Australia**
'Two of my kids left home at a young age. One left for an apprenticeship, the other married young. I found it very difficult when my 18-year-old left. I felt that he was too young but he was extremely independent. It's a difficult thing to realise that your job is done. You just have to hope and pray that the morals and values you instilled in them is enough. Mind you, they are still always your children no matter what. You just have to try and suppress the urge to tell them what to do.'

**Louise**
**Mother of one daughter aged 18 and two sons aged 13 and 9**
**From Australia**
'Give them love and do not say "yes" to everything in life. Let them experience real life and do not wrap them up in cotton wool. Teach them to trust their intuition and let go when they are doing what drives you mad. Most of all, they have to do it their way. The best you can do is love them and let them know you are there and will catch them if they fall.'

**Liz**
**Mother of two sons aged 19 and 10 and two daughters aged 8 and 5**
**From Australia.**
'It's a very steep learning curve so be ready for anything, but try to enjoy the journey too. Pick your battles and focus on the things that really matter to you, because young adults tend to tune out very quickly.

'Stay firm on the foundational beliefs that your family values are based on. Even though they will kick against this at times, I think even the surliest young adult will respect you for it. This is especially important if you still have little ones at home as it means they know you stand by your word.

'Be able to apologise when you stuff things up in your role as a parent. I think it's good for them to know that we are learning on the job. Don't forget that big 'kids' need cuddles too, even though they may seem resistant. I think my six feet tall boy needs a hug from his mum as much as my little preppie does!'

**Johannah**
**Mother of one son aged 27 and one daughter aged 23**
**From USA**
'Let them go, it's what we raise them to do ultimately. Work on cultivating your relationship with your spouse independent of the children so when that time comes, you're not left lonely and wondering.

'Encourage your kids to take risks (within reason of course) and listen, I mean *really listen* to what their dreams and aspirations are. Do not criticise or discourage. Allow them to dream big and to just know that you will be there if, not when, they fall. You will not be disappointed and watching them achieve those dreams is a gift.'

# Words of wisdom:
# Children with special needs

**Rae**
**Mother of one son aged 11 and one daughter aged 2**
**From Australia**

'You are about to embark on a journey that will open you up to a world you never knew existed. Don't be afraid. There are many beautiful, caring, like-minded women in this new world and you are not alone.

'Research as much as you can about all kinds of neuro-therapies, as there are many. It will empower you as a mother to know that you are going to be the best therapist your child has, because therapy begins in the home.

'It takes more than a couple of half-hour visits to your physio or occupational therapist to see results. You need to find a professional who will support you with an in-home program and work with you. It's going to be tough, but believe me when I tell you that it does get easier and you will find yourself again. When that day comes and your child meets those milestones, regardless of how late, it will all have been worth it and you will be a better person for it. Because the deeper the sorrow, the greater the joy.'

## Kathryn
## Mother of two sons aged 11 and 6 and one daughter aged 8
## From Australia

'I'd like to let all newly diagnosed parents know that it gets better. It gets normal. Once you get over the hump of toddler-hood, it's all up from there.

'Don't limit your child by the label and certainly don't tell everyone you meet, because they will limit your child with this information. Do not let your child define themselves with this label either.

'Raising a child with a disability is a bit like swimming out of a rip at the beach. You want to get back to the beach with everyone else, but you can't swim straight to shore. Instead, you swim across the rip. It's a different way, it's a bit longer, but you still end up on the beach.

'My kids go to a mainstream school. They go to Scouts and tennis. They have friends and they have their quirks, but they are happy, healthy and loved.'

## Emma
## Mother of two sons aged 17 and 9
## From UK

'Embrace everything your child does. Love the life they have and love them. Don't tell them that you know how it feels to be them, because you don't. Only they know that, so listen to them.

'If or when things go wrong for your child, fight for them. Let them know that you are on their side.

'Be realistic about their strengths and weaknesses, but don't hold them back or let other people's pre-conceptions hold them back. This can be a very difficult balancing act. My children have dyslexia so, re-alistically, they will never win a spelling bee competition. With a bit of help and the use of a laptop, however, they can reach their academic potential and be whoever they want to be.'

## Terri
### Mother of one daughter aged 13 and one son aged 6
### From Australia

'Children of above average intelligence have a ridiculous amount of energy that needs to be exerted. Challenge them with lots of brain stimulation like early learning reading, simple math problems and lots of physical activities such as gymnastics and music lessons.'

## Moran
### Mother of four daughters aged 10, 8, 6 and 2
### From Australia

'There've been times when one of my kids was a little 'off balance'. Things would seem much harder for them or they would get 'stuck' before transitioning to a new development. At these times, I had no hesitation in getting advice from a psychologist. Often this was just as therapeutic for me, giving me an opportunity to offload my worry or fears as well as getting practical advice on how to manage difficult situations.

'Be kind to yourself. It's tough down there in the trenches. Treat yourself as you would your best friend. You can only do the best you can and if you can't, go get some advice on how to make your life a little easier. It's OK to say, "This is hard, I don't know what to do".'

## Akshaya
### Mother of one daughter aged 4 and one son aged 1
### From Australia

'I strongly believe that children with high intellectual potential also need support, encouragement and guidance as they have not yet mastered the art of using their genetic skills to optimum levels. They should get access to resources and opportunities to grow without being labeled as 'gifted'. Kids are vulnerable at both ends of the spectrum.'

## Paulina
### Mother of three daughters aged 14, 11 and 9
### From Malaysia

'As a parent, you need to let go of the idea of the 'ideal' child. When my second daughter was born with down syndrome, I had to learn to live with her abilities. I had to un-learn the idea of what I'd imagined her to be. I had to learn to let her be who she is, to love her for who she is. I realised that if I kept hanging on to that ideal, I would be disappointed in her, in myself and in our lives in general.'

## Jane
### Mother of two daughters aged 19 and 17 and one son aged 5
### From UK

'Stop punishing yourself by thinking that this is somehow your fault. They were born to be who they are supposed to be. This is your child's path of life, their soul journey. They came into the world this way so they can get what they need to get from this lifetime.

'I often find myself worrying about what someone else thinks of my little boy and his sudden meltdowns. During these times, I feel all eyes are on me and that my parenting skills are being judged. I am learning to not give a damn, it's their ignorance. Repeat these latter thoughts to empower yourself, many times over if it helps you to overcome angst.

'Parenting a child who doesn't fit inside the box is so hard but also incredibly amazing. When you go through the tough times that make you feel as though you want to just fold, then have these times replaced by amazing moments where you see your child's unique view on life— it completely takes your breath away. Stay focused on that!

'Lastly, know that everything is unfolding exactly as it should be. Have faith in the universe and know that you are supported. Let go of what's dragging you down, such as fear, worry or frustration. Don't be afraid to be your child's voice. You are simply that, doing the best you can in decision-making about your child's well-being and future.

'People 'in the know' tell me it will get better, that it's merely a journey of self-discovery for both yourself and your child. Keep coming back to these beliefs whenever you feel the need to. I do!'

Mandy
Mother of three daughters being twins aged 9 and one 3-year-old
From Australia

'You will have chronic sorrow. It's a sadness that will stay with you for the rest of your life. Knowing this though helps you to move through, accept and sit with the sadness.

'Know that you know how to love deeply through sacrifice. You will become a fierce lover of your child, so fierce that it can knock you over.

'Dress your special needs child like a prince or princess. Shower them with the best that you can afford. This is in your control. Present them to the world with great pride.

'When you are ready and comfortable, get respite. You will need this. Find the people in your 'tribe'. Seek out others who are in similar situations, then you will no longer feel in a minority. Rather, you will belong as best you can.

'Know that you would change this situation for your child, but maybe not for yourself because you have learnt the greatest lesson on earth—love.'

Theresa
Mother of two sons aged 11 and 6 and one daughter aged 8
From USA

'Have patience in understanding that their world is vastly different from yours. Your ability to be the calm through their storms is essential to their growth and positive well-being.'

Caroline
Mother of two sons aged 6 and 3 and one daughter aged 1
From UK

'Never lose sight of the fact that your child is a person, not a list of characteristics or symptoms written in a leaflet or textbook. Your child will be more like you and your family than any other child with the same condition.

'I missed so many precious moments by worrying unnecessarily about our future together and I would do anything to hold my precious newborn in my arms again with the feelings I have now. We lead a really rewarding, typical family life together and you will too.

'I truly believe that inclusion in schools, sport, communities, media and society is the key to acceptance. By growing up with 'difference', we will breed a new generation who see people as people and not labels. Our children are our best tool in changing attitudes and removing outdated stereotypes, just by being themselves—and by being included.'

### Alison
### Mother of two sons aged 10 and 6 and one daughter aged 3
### From Australia

'Our first-born was born fighting for his life and has many challenges. With that, motherhood has been a very different experience on so many levels.

'There have been many painful days of grief, of questioning why. Why was he born with so many difficulties and why do I have to go through all of this? But without this experience, I wouldn't be the mum that I am.

'I learned to surrender to the fact that life doesn't always live up to your expectations and I love quotes, so I am always finding ones to fit in with how I feel. "This too shall pass", is a good one because all things in life, whether good or bad, are fleeting and changing all the time. You have to take the good with the bad. No matter what, love is all that matters.'

### Vicki
### Mother of one daughter aged 9
### From UK

'It's hard, but you have to accept that it's just the way your child is. You can't change it. You have to look for the positives in everything thrown at you. At every hospital visit, you have to be proud about how brave they are. You have to be good to yourself too and tell yourself that everything will be alright. You don't love them any less, the way you feel as their mother doesn't change. It's just the way they are.'

# Words of wisdom:
# Post-natal depression

**Kellie**
**Mother of one son aged 1**
**From Australia**
'This is a topic that I feel people avoid like the plague. I did experience this mildly. I experienced anxiety a lot more than depression, but I didn't experience either until my son was about eight months old.

'The one thing I did learn was that *it's ok to say,"I'm not ok"*. Seek help. It doesn't mean you're a nutcase, it means you're human. Talk! Sometimes just getting things off your chest does the world of good. I found that the more I opened up to people, the better I felt. I was also surprised at the amount of people who had been through the same as me or were dying for someone to talk to also.'

**Merryn**
**Mother of one son aged 8 and one daughter aged 3**
**From Australia**
'Remember to breathe and connect with your heart in moments of depression or anxiety, as the mind takes you away from your heart's centre.

'Connect with people you feel comfortable opening up to and tell them what's going on inside your mind. They won't judge you for being honest.'

### Terri
### Mother of one daughter aged 13 and one son aged 6
### From Australia

'Having suffered from post-natal depression, all I can say is forget the housework, trust your instincts, get plenty of sleep where you can, ask for help, accept help offered and eat wholesome nutritious food. If you try to be a superwoman, things only get worse. Your baby is only a newborn once, so enjoy that period without putting too much pressure on yourself.'

### Tegan
### Mother of one daughter aged 6 and one son aged 3
### From Australia

'It's not normal to feel flat and as though everything is impossible. If you feel like this, talk to someone: your partner, friends, neighbour or doctor. It's the hardest thing to do but it's the best thing you can do for yourself and your baby.

'I'm a better mum for dealing with my post-natal depression and getting on top of my emotions. When I'm happy and in control, the kids are happy and the house is happy!'

### Patrycja
### Mother of two daughters aged 7 and 5 and one son aged 3
### From Switzerland

'Having a child is one of the most magical, beautiful, joyful experiences in the world. It is also a moment of tremendous transformation as we move into vast unknown territory and a world riddled with advice and opinions about everything.

'After having this child in our belly for nine months, we hold this precious being in our arms and can suddenly feel totally helpless. The floods of emotions along with the physical demands of motherhood require super powers—and all at once. All too often, we feel completely and utterly unprepared. Despite being surrounded by well-meaning (but often misguided) advice from people and books, we find ourselves feeling totally alone on this journey.

'These are all feelings that so many mamas experience and find too hard to share: the lack of sleep, the uncertainty and the feeling that everyone else seems to have figured 'it' out (insert breast feeding, sleep, diaper rash, eczema, allergies, green poop, poor latch, insufficient milk supply and so on). With all these come the feelings of guilt, of not being good enough, of frustration and loneliness in our silence. Yet you are not alone. Reach out and find others to know that this journey is a learning curve for us all, each of us equally inexperienced and full of personal wisdom as the other.

'The spectrum of such feelings as a new baby arrives is often masked by hormones and lack of sleep, yet the feelings are real. For some, the support of a good friend is enough. For others, more is needed and there is no shame in asking for help to get ourselves through the difficult moments.'

Tayler
**Mother of one son aged 3**
**From USA**
'After the birth of my son, I was the happiest and saddest I've ever been. It was confusing and terrifying and I felt so helpless. This went on for three months before I had a full-blown panic attack, complete with a trip to the ER. After this, my husband and I had a conversation and I told him I needed help, that I couldn't get out of this place alone. He suggested I seek counseling. This was the best decision I could have made for myself and for my family.

'Being in counseling helped me to tackle issues that had been buried deep since childhood. Maybe it was the hormonal shift or the pure exhaustion that meant I could no longer keep all of it stuffed down. My advice to any mommas out there who think they might be facing these issues is to get help! It is not your fault and getting help will be the best thing for you, your baby and your family. You are loved and supported by a wonderful group of moms out there who have come before you, many of who have also dealt with depression and are silently cheering you on.'

Beccy
**Mother of one daughter aged 21 and three sons aged 4, 2 and 11 months**
**From Australia**
'I didn't even notice that I had post-natal depression (PND). It was my husband who picked up on it. I did not want to leave the house or interact with people. I went to the doctor and got onto anti-depressants. After two to three weeks, I started to feel a lot better. I definitely needed to eat healthy though and force myself to go for a walk or even just sit outside in the sun.

'I found that online mummy group sites were a great way to connect with other women who had PND also. I found it was ok to share my PND with some people, but my husband and I decided not to disclose it to others who didn't understand it. We knew they wouldn't have been supportive and support is what you need. Some days are harder than others but remember, you are not alone.'

Joanna
**Mother of one daughter aged 6 and one son aged 2**
**From Canada**
'If you stop recognising yourself; when it becomes too difficult to move, breath or do anything; if you stop seeing the light—please find courage and ask for help. You need it and you deserve it. Remember that you are not alone, you are loved!'

# Words of wisdom:
# General tips

Amanda de Cadenet
Mother of two daughters aged 22 and 7 and one son aged 7
Television Personality, Renowned Photographer and Entrepreneur
From UK
'I think it's really important that my boy learn how to treat women with respect, dignity and kindness. I think it's important that my daughter be able to see her mother as someone who is her mom and my primary role in life is as her mom, but second of all as a businesswoman. I run my business. I'm self-supporting. My job is what contributes to paying for her school fees. I'm not reliant on her dad to pay for our house and buy her clothes.

'I hope that my son and daughter see that I'm somebody who's a balanced woman, someone who's kind and thoughtful but who also teaches them boundaries and alternatives when they go wrong. Of course, I don't know how to do this perfectly. I'm just winging it and learning as I go, because anybody who fronts like they've got it down is not telling you the truth. Nobody does.'

Cinnamon
Mother of four daughters aged 13, 11, 10 and 7 and one son aged 8
From Australia
'They say trust has to be earned but with your children, I feel like trust

only has to be earned if it has been broken first. When that baby is placed in your arms, all of their trust is in you. They trust that you will keep them safe, fed and loved. They trust you completely, without even realising it.

'Then, as they grow and venture out on their own, you trust them. This happens first in little ways, like walking in the shops instead of being trapped in the pram, then heading off to pre-school all alone and eventually off to school. You trust that they will behave and treat people the way you have taught them to.

'As they get older, you have to release the apron strings more and more. I have found that in trusting my children, they trust me in return. This means we can talk about anything, which means there is always understanding and that means they don't have to lie to do what they want.

'So the best advice I have to give is to trust your children. If you are raising them to the best of your ability then what reason would there be to not trust them from the outset? After all, you are their greatest role model.'

## Sabine
**Mother of two daughters aged 25 and 11 and two sons aged 22 and 16**
**From Germany**

'When you can't sleep properly because every night, something is going on in the kids' rooms—they are thirsty or teething, the cuddly toy has fallen out of their bed or they've had a nightmare. When you don't get enough sleep, so you're not able to even imagine how it is to be well-rested. When you think you're just too exhausted to get up several times during the night. When all this happens, remind yourself what a gift it is to mean the world to someone. Just to be held in your arms solves every problem for someone. Just to be held in your arms is the only thing that someone needs. How great is that? I can tell you that you will long for these moments when your children grow older, so try to *enjoy* this part of motherhood—even if you are so tired.'

Louise
Mother of one son aged 5 and one daughter aged 3
From UK

'Don't compare yourself to other mums. Every family dynamic is different. Other mums might look like they are 'super mum', but no-one knows their story. We all do the best job we can to love, nurture, educate and inspire our children. No comparisons are necessary.'

Jools Oliver
Mother of three daughters aged 12, 11 and 5 and one son aged 3
Children's Clothing Designer and Author
From UK

'Since becoming parents Jamie and I have, more often than not, found ourselves in some ridiculous, stressful, traumatic and rather embarrassing situations involving the children.

'Your emotions are tested daily to their limits, generally swinging from extreme happiness to intense frustration and anger. I absolutely adore my job as a mum, but I don't know of any other profession whose daily curriculum can involve tears, laughter, constant negotiations, bargaining, begging and picking up the same things over and over again—plus demands for an extreme amount of patience. Some of these skills I have definitely had to learn over the last 12 years and am still learning, even now.

'I feel I am still not wise enough yet, as every second of every day I learn something new and beautiful. Each new piece of learning is such a precious gift that makes me eternally grateful to be a parent and a mum to my four special children. It's an ongoing journey that I feel extremely privileged to be on. So if you are about to take on this great expedition with my little bit of insight into motherhood, for God's sake please try and keep a sense of humour. You will need it!'

Nicole
Mother of two sons aged 7 and 5 and one daughter aged 2
From Australia

'Be consistent. Set your rules, whatever they may be and consistently expect that behaviour. Set high expectations from the start. Kids are so smart and will surprise you.

'My other tip is to look after yourself and be kind to yourself. You will inevitably be able to cope better with all the challenges that mums are faced with.'

### Helen
### Mother of one daughter aged 3
### From UK

'One piece of advice I would give to any parent of a one-year-old who is starting to take on new challenges is, be positive. I know that sounds simple to some or impossible to others but seriously, when you get down to seeing the world through your toddler's eyes, it makes you realise how scary this world is and why they rely on us as parents so much. We are our child's guidance and support and we must get the balance right between being over-protective and setting them up for a fall.

'So how have I taken on that challenge? I've made every experience a positive one. Every time my daughter gives me a look to see how I'm enjoying the experience, I always smile and laugh. Children pick up on our moods and reactions so easily. If they see you are worried, then they will be and they won't even know why.

'I apply this positive attitude to everything, from tiny things such as being splashed by another child in a swimming pool to falling over. I'm certainly not saying I'm unsympathetic, I just move my child's attention away from the negative situation to a more positive one. Or I embrace the situation, like the splashing in the swimming pool. I laugh it off and say, "That's so much fun. You can splash Mommy if you like".

'Now whether this is all a coincidence I don't know (we'll soon see with baby number two as I'm 31 weeks pregnant) but my daughter embraces all new experiences with a positive attitude. I'm not saying she throws herself in head first, but she's always willing to give everything a try with a big smile on her face. She knows her mommy and daddy are there to make sure she is safe, but she also knows she can try everything without having any fears imposed by our negative experiences in life. Children need to try things out for themselves with a positive attitude to ensure it becomes a positive experience. As parents, we need to guide and support them with a positive outlook ourselves.'

Jane Kennedy
**Mother of one daughter aged 13 and four sons aged 11, 10 and twin 7-year-olds**
**Media Personality**
**From Australia**

'I don't know about you, but it's not easy to come by compliments these days. So here's a really easy way to feel good about yourself and about being a parent. It might not happen every time, but the strike rate's pretty high. So here it is: cook a kid one of their favorite meals. I know it sounds daggy, old fashioned and 1950s home-makery, but I feel pretty buzzed every time one of my guys says, "That was *so* yum, Mum". Sometimes it can be the high point in a lousy day!

'I'm not talking about creating some insane gourmet concoction. My guys' favorite meals are super easy, like scrambled eggs and bacon, tuna pasta or roast chook. It's never the same if someone else cooks those dishes for them. It's all about the way *you* do it.

'So don't underestimate the power of the fry pan—and don't cheat yourself out of a compliment.'

Becky
**Mother of two sons aged 6 and 3**
**From Australia**

'My auntie told me three days after I had my first son, "Anyone who says having children is easy is either lying or can't remember". This has always stuck with me and helped when I have had to listen to those mums whose children are hitting every target and ticking every box while I felt like I was drowning. Motherhood is hard, so hard, but so wonderful.'

Esther
Mother of two daughters aged 9 and 4 and two sons aged 7 and 1
From the Netherlands
'When you're going through a difficult moment with your children, try to change the scenery. Just take everyone outside for a little walk, play a game in another part of the house or have a bath. Even if you're in the middle of making dinner, just grab a snack and spend half an hour doing something else. The break will make everyone feel better—and dinner can wait.'

Emma
Mother of two sons aged 17 and 9
From UK
'Read the books, listen to advice, research on the internet—but then stop. Put the books away. Switch off the computer. Forget (most) of what you have learned. Your child is amazing, unique and yours. No-one has ever written a book about your child. At the end of the day, this little human will not have read the books, listened to the advice or searched the internet for how to behave and develop. Trust your instincts, listen to your head and your heart and trust that, most of the time, you will know exactly what to do.

'Hugs are magic. They cure heartache, cut knees, nasty friends, horrid teachers, bad days, tummy ache, bad dreams and much more. Never, ever underestimate the power of the hug.

'Don't be afraid to let them grow up. Each year, each month, each day brings new experiences. There is as much to learn from a 17 year old, just as there is from a seven year old. Every stage heralds new adventures. Just make sure you make the time to enjoy these with them.

'We all get it wrong, quite often. Sometimes we make monumental cock-ups. This is normal and doesn't make you a bad parent. Try to learn from your mistakes and keep doing your best. If you do get it wrong, don't be afraid to apologise to your child. You want them to apologise to you, so lead by example.'

Patrycja
**Mother of two daughters aged 7 and 5 and one son aged 3**
**From Switzerland**
'No matter how busy our days get, my family always tries to sit down and eat at least one daily meal together (not always easy with competing schedules). I can only imagine it will get more and more challenging as the kids get older. Yet it's at meals that we have the opportunity to sit together and engage without distraction.

'I remember my mom telling me once that she was always too busy to sit down to eat and as a child, I would always ask her to sit with us. Only as I grew did she realise what she'd missed. So it's wisdom I learned from her, which I cherish deeply.

'At the meals we eat together, there is only one dual rule: we are kind and respectful with each other, with ourselves and with our food. If someone does not want to eat, that's okay. They can just sit and be with us. Funnily enough, even our pickiest eater usually forgets to be fussy and enjoys her meals when we don't focus on the food itself.

'Patience is always a tough one for me. So often, I feel like I am the only one who loses it from time to time (some days more than others). So often, I feel like if only I had my mama around I could turn to her for that solid support and breathe through the chaos into the next moment. Of course the more I talk to other moms, the more I know I am not alone. Though every time I have to dig deeper and deeper for that extra dose of patience, I doubt myself and my ability to be a 'good parent'. While this does not seem like any kind of words of wisdom, the pearl for me is in sharing. Whether it's patience, or any other quality that we mamas believe we are not doing 'enough' of. By talking with each other we realise that we are not alone and that it's okay. It's all part of the journey, especially for those of us who do not have our own mamas to turn to in those difficult moments. We are not alone.'

Marguerite
**Mother of twin sons aged 21 and one daughter aged 19**
**From Australia**
'The teenage years are hard ones for parents. For the entirety of your

child's life, your focus has been highly on protecting and keeping them safe. All of a sudden, this ability starts to slip away.

'At age 16, many teenagers get their Learner's license and many hours are spent teaching them how to drive. By 17, they may have their Provisional licence and be on the road. They will also be getting in the car with their friends driving. Once teenagers hit 18, you will inevitably hear the words, "I am 18, I can do what I want". The safety of your children is no longer within your total control. These are the years where you must trust that your morals and values have become instilled in your children and that they have good common sense. These are the years in which your worries and anxieties could get the better of you. You must try and find a way to control them. The mobile phone is your friend. A simple text message from your child to let you know they have arrived at a destination, or that they are on their way home, can be so very reassuring. Help them to understand that a quick text message provides enormous reassurance to you. Hopefully they will be happy to oblige and get into the habit of sending those reassuring texts.'

**Lisa Wilkinson**
**Mother of two sons aged 20 and 18 and one daughter aged 16**
**Co-host of 'The Today Show'**
**From Australia**
'As a parent, you're never going to be the only influence in your child's life—so you've got to try and be the best. I'm a great believer that children learn their greatest, most lasting lessons from us when we think they're not watching. And they always are.'

**Dallas**
**Mother of two sons aged 10 and 6**
**From Canada**
'Sometimes when they are little, you have days when you can't wait until they are older so that things are easier or whatever. Then all of a sudden, they are big and you want them too be little again. Don't wish the days away.'

Jill
Mother of one son aged 16 and two daughters aged 14 and 12
From Australia

'If you want your kids to grow up with confidence and to be happy and successful, show them it's important to take time out to pamper yourself. As a mum, we often give to everyone first and to ourselves last. But you can't give to others what you don't have, so fill your own cup up first.'

Moran
Mother of four daughters aged 10, 8, 6 and 2
From Australia

'I am very, very strict about bedtime in my house. With four kids, this is important. I love my kids, but I don't want to hang out with them at night. After 7.30pm it's adult time. Why? Because. Goodnight.'

Deborah Thomas
Mother of one son aged 12
Magazine Editor
From Australia

'The way I am with my son is very much how my mother was with me. Unconditional love in spades accompanied by a deep understanding of what is right and wrong, respect for others and a belief that if you work hard and put your mind to it, you can do and be anything.

'As someone who had her child later in life, in my mid-40s, Oscar has brought unimaginable joy and fulfillment into my world. Every day, I let him know that he is my gift from the gods. On occasion I can feel a little guilty when work takes me away, but my husband tells me to not sweat the small stuff and to look at my relationship with Oscar in the context of a lifetime. Like Mum, who also worked when I was growing up, I will always be there when he needs me and he knows that. He is my number one priority and I love spending time with him. He makes me laugh and watching him evolve into an independent teenager with his own ideas and interests is truly rewarding. But no matter what, I still expect him to behave and he gets that.

'Looking back, I think Vitek and I set the boundaries around acceptable behaviour when Oscar was very young. That's when the learning begins and it is important to be consistent and clear with your child so that throughout your life together, you can gently guide them to do and be their best.'

## Lu
### Mother of two daughters aged 13 and 8
### From Australia

'Every day during our evening meal, we do something called 'favourite parts of the day'. Each person gets a turn at talking about their favourite part of their day. No-one is to interrupt the speaker. It encourages articulation, reflection, insight into the day's events and communication. If it's been a bad day with no favourite part then we change the question to, "What are you grateful for?".'

## Brenda
### Mother of one son aged 8 and one daughter aged 6
### From Australia

'Now that you are a mother, you'll naturally want to put your children first all the time. This is great in theory, however, make sure you look after yourself too. You can do this in many ways. Connecting with other mums is great, so join a mothers group, playgroup or free sessions at your local library. Time away from your children is just as important and can simply be a few hours each week to get yourself rejuvenated.

'If you can't get regular time away, go for a walk with your babies in a pram, attend a mums and bubs movie session or, once you're connected with some other mums in your community, take turns in caring for each others' children every now and again. It really does help. A happy mum means a happy family.'

Georgie Gardner
Mother of one daughter aged 9 and one son aged 7
Television Journalist
From Australia

'As a mother who has always combined paid work with parenting, there are fewer contact hours to be together. I have, therefore, always tried my hardest to be 'present'. In my experience, children want our time more than anything else. So when they ask me to partake in colouring in or jumping on the trampoline, or maybe sorting through soccer cards, I make a point of making that my priority. Folding the washing, peeling the vegetables or responding to an email can all wait. Being 'in the moment' and appreciative of being asked to partake are both things to be cherished and valued. It is a finite period that we will never get back. You might also be surprised by how much fun it is!'

Jackie
Mother of two daughters aged 27 and 25 and one son aged 23
From Australia

'As a mother, I always found that one of the most special things for me was seeing my young children react and respond when I told them how beautiful and amazing they were. Children need to hear positive things about themselves and this boost of self-esteem is so important, I believe. So tell your children they are beautiful and tell them that you love them every day. This was something my mum instilled in me as I grew up. Feeling loved is something every child deserves.'

Lauren
Mother of one son aged 10 and two daughters aged 8 and 4
From Australia

'For any girl, woman, sister, mother, aunt or grandmother, if you know that you're doing your best, you are. You have the ability to find the beauty in any situation because we're only given what we can handle. Go forth within your greatness. Be proud for who you are and who you've grown to be, of your story and the privilege you have of growing and moulding your own children. Pick your women wisely and support, empower and uplift each other, always. Be brave and challenge yourself in this one life you have. Believe you can and you will.'

# Acknowledgements

So, here I sit, ready to complete what seems like the final piece of the puzzle, at the end of one of the most emotional and exciting rides of my life and I have so many people to thank for helping me get to this stage!

First and foremost, to my wonderfully patient husband Tim. Honestly, I think that you are a saint! You continue to put up with me *and* my grand ideas and you push me along to reach my goals when I feel like throwing in the towel! You are my absolute rock and my best friend and I am just so lucky that the universe arranged for us to collide! I love you ever so much. You + Me = Awesome xxx

To my darling, delicious, supportive boys. Oh you all make me SO proud. Your Nan would think that you are all just the best children walking this earth!! I thank you all for being supportive of me while my head was choc full of book related info and forgiving me for my scattery brain during this mad adventure. I sure got lucky with the 4 of you. I love you all to the moon and back a billion times over. I hope that I have made you proud. xxx

To my Sisterhood of seriously amazing friends. Through thick and thin, we all support and encourage each other and it has been such a gorgeous ride so far growing older and wiser with you all. You know the saying 'surround yourself with those who lift you higher...'?, well, I have and you all do. I thank you for listening to my incessant ramblings about this dream of mine for the past few years and for your unwavering support. I am a very lucky girl and I love you all so much. I can only imagine the future girls nights when we are all old and grey.

Look out world!! XX

To the very generous Jools Oliver for believing in me and my dream of creating this book from conception. I am so grateful for the advice you have given me along the way and for raising awareness of certain needs that have come about as the writing process ticked along. Your willingness to help others is admirable. xx

To my family, thank you for your ongoing encouragement and support. You have all been on this ride with me since we learnt of the sad news regarding Mums illness and have supported me all the way. I'm thrilled to have been able to include family in my book. I hope you love it. XX

Of course, a huge thank you must go out to all of the amazing people who have been involved in the creation of this book.

The very talented Sarah Lord of 'Sarah Lord Papercuts' who created the stunning images that bind this book together. We just clicked and you knew exactly what I was hoping to achieve and you nailed it! You truly are fabulous. Thank you xx.

Photographer extraordinaire Katie Toland of 'Katie Toland Photography' for the stunning cover images. You are a pure joy to work with and I am so grateful that you saw the same vision for the cover as I did! Next book, consider the cover as your blank canvas!

To my gorgeous friend Bec of 'Rebecca Vaughan Make-Up Artist' who has become my self-appointed Make-Up magician and is responsible for the face that appears on the back cover! You my dear are just so good at what you do! You manage to transform my tired, mother of 4, weary face into someone that I just don't recognise, but LOVE. I adore make-up playtime time, its just too much fun, and so much laughter.

To the lovely Sarah Wayland for contributing her foreword to this book. You string words together so beautifully and I am very grateful for your support. It's been a pleasure to work with you.

Most importantly, to all of the beautiful mothers who have taken the time to contribute amazing, touching and inspiring words. You should all be very proud of yourselves for caring and therefore brightening the lives of Motherless Mothers worldwide. I have experienced firsthand the true sense of a Sisterhood whilst creating this book and I am so proud to be a part of a strong and encouraging village of mothers. I'm eternally grateful. XXX

Finally to my readers, I thank you so much for picking this book up and giving it a chance. My wish as you prepare to close it, is that you are feeling a sense of calm and hope. I hope that you feel further connected to other Motherless Mums and know that you are not alone in your ongoing journey without your mother. Stay strong. Stay positive and be proud.

Much love, always,
Leigh Van Der Horst. xxxx

To remain connected, please visit **www.leighvloves.com**

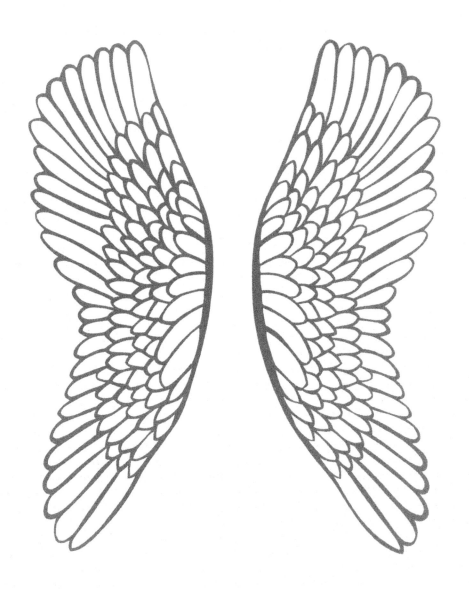

LEIGH VAN DER HORST is the wife of a wonderful man and mother to four boys. They live on Victoria's beautiful Mornington Peninsula. Leigh discovered a passion for writing when her beloved mother passed away from cancer and can often be found writing for her website 'Leigh V Loves'.

Email: leighvanderhorst@gmail.com
Website: www.leighvloves.com
Facebook: www.facebook.com/sixbythebay
Instagram: www.instagram.com/leighvanderhorst

Lightning Source UK Ltd.
Milton Keynes UK
UKOW04f0628250118
316812UK00002B/100/P